THE CATHOLIC UNIVERSITY OF AMERICA
CANON LAW STUDIES
Number 60

DOMICILE AND QUASI-DOMICILE

A DISSERTATION

Submitted to the Faculty of Canon Law of the Catholic University of America in Partial Fulfilment of the Requirements for the Degree of

DOCTOR OF CANON LAW

BY THE

REVEREND JOHN M. COSTELLO, A.B., J.C.L.
Priest of the Archdiocese of New York

THE CATHOLIC UNIVERSITY OF AMERICA
WASHINGTON, D. C.
1930

Nihil Obstat:

PHILIPPUS BERNARDINI, S. T. D., J. U. D.,
Censor Deputatus.
Washingtonii, D. C., die xxvii Maii, 1930.

Imprimatur:

✠ PATRITIUS CARDINALIS HAYES,
Archiepiscopus Neo Eboracensis.
Neo Eboraci, die xxxi Maii, 1930.

WASHINGTON TYPOGRAPHERS, INC.
WASHINGTON, D. C.

TABLE OF CONTENTS

PAGE

PART II

Present Legislation

FOREWORD

So intimate is the bearing of domicile and quasi-domicile upon the exercise of many Christian rights and obligations that a study of these institutions can never be without interest for ecclesiastical readers. Subjection to the law of a particular territory and to the jurisdiction of local superiors depends to a very great extent on domicile and quasi-domicile. These factors also play an important part in determining one's proper pastor and ordinary for the reception of the sacraments, and many other matters of ecclesiastical discipline. In addition to the many practical considerations connected with the question of domicile and quasi-domicile, the antiquity of these institutions, particularly of the domicile, renders them important from an historical standpoint.

In the present dissertation, after tracing their historical development, the general principles of domicile and quasi-domicile will be discussed.

The writer takes this occasion to express his gratitude to the members of the faculty of the School of Canon Law for their generous direction and assistance throughout the course of studies and in the preparation of this dissertation. He also acknowledges his indebtedness to the Reverend Edward Sweeney, A.M., of Brooklyn, for invaluable suggestions and guidance.

PART I—HISTORICAL DEVELOPMENT

CHAPTER I

DOMICILE IN ROMAN LAW

In general, the extent of one's legal capacity in Roman Law depended on one's civil position or status. This was viewed with reference to three things, viz., *libertas*, or personal freedom; *civitas*, or citizenship; *familia*, or domestic position.[1]

For our purpose, the extremely important question of citizenship will be our chief concern. Three points are to be distinguished: (1) Rome, the *communis patria*, where a person was a *civis Romanus*, and enjoyed the *jus civitatis*; (2) the local city, where a person was a *municeps*, and enjoyed the *jus originis*; (3) domicile, where a person was an *incola*, and enjoyed the *jus domicilii*. The first section has been introduced to afford some historical background, and to show in just what sphere of Roman life the Roman *origo* and its legal extension, the domicile, came into play.

Article I.—Roman Citizenship

In ancient Rome, before the era of trustworthy history begins, one can view the question of citizenship with little more than conjecture. The earliest

[1] R. W. Leage, *Roman Private Law*, p. 44; W. W. Buckland, *A Manual of Roman Private Law*, p. 34.

social and political institution of the Italian peoples was known as the *gens*. This institution seems to have been an association of families descended from a common ancestor, and it formed, it may be said, a small-sized state. To be a member (citizen) of a *gens*, it was necessary that one be an agnatic descendant of an eponymous ancestor, and that his connection with this ancestor exist in an unbroken line. The body of rights which the members of the *gens* enjoyed was called the *jus gentilitatis*.[2]

In the course of time, the gradual union of the pre-existing *gentes* formed the early Roman state. It may be noted here that, with the establishment of the state, the period of actual history begins. Naturally enough, citizenship in this early Roman state was possessed only by those who were descendants of the members of the early *gentes* of which the state was composed, viz., the patricians. Together with the patricians, however, there existed in the early Roman state another class of people called the plebeians. It is not within our province to discuss the origin of this class. Suffice it to say that in the beginning its members did not possess the rights which the patricians enjoyed. There were, then, in the early Roman state, two classes of people: patricians, possessing full civic rights, and plebeians, possessing no civic rights, a distinction paralleled in later times by the distinction between *cives Romani* and *peregrini*.[3] After a struggle of about two hundred years the plebeians finally achieved a legal position in Rome equal to that of the patricians.

To this union of the patricians and plebeians into

[2] J. Declareuil, *Rome the Law Giver*, p. 38 ff.

[3] R. W. Leage, *Roman Private Law*, p. 14.

one political society is ascribed the origin of the notion of *civitas*, and the *jus civitatis*, i.e., the body of rights possessed by Roman citizens and denied to foreigners. The *jus civitatis* included public rights, viz., the right to vote and to hold office, and private rights, viz., the right to intermarriage and to possess and dispose of property with legal protection.[4] Full citizenship consisted of the possession of both public and private rights. Partial citizenship embraced only private rights.

At about the time the plebeians achieved civil equality with the patricians, Rome, as a result of the Latin and Italian wars, had become mistress of Italy, and in her relations with the conquered towns can be noted an extension of the *jus civitatis*. Although Italy was united under the Roman hegemony, it by no means formed a single state. It was not the policy of Rome to annex the conquered cities and rule them directly. On the contrary, the Roman policy was to isolate the different cities, permit local self-government and grant them a partial citizenship.[5] The inhabitants of these cities enjoying partial citizenship were called Latins, and their legal condition was called *Latinitas* as opposed to *civitas*. Thus we see that by the middle of the third century B. C., all Italy outside of Rome was literally dotted with communities whose inhabitants enjoyed self-government and a varied citizenship.

The middle of the second century B. C. saw the

[4] W. C. Morey, *Outlines of Roman Law*, pp. 48–49.

[5] Savigny, *System des heutigen Römischen Rechts*, VIII, §351. Full citizenship was granted to some towns, but it seems that the majority possessed only partial citizenship. Cf. J. E. Sandys, *A Companion to Latin Studies*, pp. 366–7.

establishment of the universal power of Rome with the fall of Carthage. This extension of power outside of Italy was attended by the constitution of the provincial system. The provinces, though at fisrt having their own peculiar organization, gradually assumed a condition similar to Italy and the Italian towns.[6] Politically, however, the provincials were in a less favorable condition than the inhabitants of the Italian towns, as they possessed no status whatsoever as Roman citizens.[7]

Thus, at this time (towards the end of the Republic), there were three classes of people in the Roman Empire: Roman citizens, or those possessing full citizenship; Latins, or those possessing partial citizenship; and *peregrini*, who were not citizens at all.[8] In the course of time these distinctions gradually disappeared. Full citizenship was granted to the Latins, as a result of the social wars, by the *leges Julia* (90 B.C.) and *Plauta Papiria* (89 B.C.)[9] By an edict of the Emperor Caracalla issued in 212 A. D., full citizenship was bestowed on all free provincial subjects of the Roman Empire.[10] Two classes were excepted from this privilege, viz., *Latini Juniani*[11] and *Dedititii*.[12] Justinian abolished these two classes, and henceforth all free subjects of the Roman Empire were Roman citizens.[13]

---

[6] Savigny, *l. c.;* Whittuck-Poste, *Gai Institutiones Juris Civilis*, p. 296.

[7] C. P. Sherman, *Roman Law in the Modern World*, II, 31.

[8] C. P. Sherman, *l. c.*

[9] R. W. Leage, *Roman Private Law*, p. 65; C. P. Sherman, *l. c.*

[10] D. 1. 5. 17.

[11] Cf. G. 1. 13.

[12] G. 1. 21, 22.

[13] C. VII. 6. 1—R. W. Leage, *Roman Private Law*, p. 66; W. W. Buckland, *A Manual of Roman Private Law*, p. 59.

ARTICLE II.—LOCAL CITIZENSHIP: THE ROMAN *Origo*

From the above sketch, it is clear that, during the late Republic and the early Empire, the political organization of the Mediterranean world, under the domination of Rome, made the Roman Empire a federation of citizens or municipalities to which the names *civitas*, *municipium* and *colonia* were generally given.[14] These municipalities formed self-governing communities within the Empire, using their own laws,[15] having their own magistrates [16] and jurisdiction [17] and enjoying their own rights.[18] As a result of this singular organization, every free inhabitant of the Roman Empire was either a citizen of Rome or of one of the local municipalities, or of them both.

The citizens of these local municipalities, during the period of classical law, were called *municipes*.[19] In the time of Justinian, however, when every free inhabitant of the Roman world was a Roman Citizen,

---

[14] For the difference in name and the reasons for the difference, cf. J. E. Sandys, *A Companion to Latin Studies*, p. 366 ff.; Savigny, *o. c.* §352; Declareuil, *o. c. p.* 54.

[15] Aulus Gellius, *Atticae Noctes*, XVI, 13; G. Bry, *Principes de droit Romain*, p. 59; Savigny, *System*, VIII, §347.

[16] D. L. 1. 25; D. L. 1. 26; D. L. 1. 28.

[17] D. L. 1. 29; Savigny, *o. c.*, §351.

[18] Aulus Gellius, *Atticae Noctes*, XVI, 13; Savigny, *l. c.*

[19] D. L. 1. 1. "Et proprie quidem municipes appellantur muneris participes, recepti in civitatem ut munera nobiscum facerent. Sed nunc abusive municipes dicimus suae cujusque civitatis civis, utputa Campanos, Puteolanos." According to Ulpian, in the beginning, only those were called municipes who shared burdens (munera) with the Roman people; hence the name municipes (munus, capere). Afterwards citizens of any city other than Rome were called municipes. Cf. J. Cujas, *Opera Omnia*, I, 769; IV, 788; VIII, 607. Cf. also Aulus Gellius, *Atticae Noctes*, XVI, 13.

the word *civis* was applied to all.[20] Since the rights and duties of citizenship varied in the different cities, it was important to determine the city to which one belonged.[21]

§1. *Acquisition of Citizenship*

Citizenship in a local municipality, during the classical period of Roman law, could be acquired in three ways, viz., by birth, manumission and adoption. *Municipem aut nativitas facit, aut manumissio, aut adoptio.*[22] In Justinian law, a fourth way of acquiring citizenship was added, viz., *adlectio. Cives quidem origo, manumissio, allectio vel adoptio.*[23]

Birth (*nativitas, origo*). This was the usual way of acquiring citizenship. The general principle in Roman law was that, in a legal marriage (*justae nuptiae*), the child followed the *origo* of his father.[24] It was not the actual place of birth that determined one's *origo*. The legal birthplace was the decisive test, i.e., the place where the father had the *jus originis*, and where ordinarily the child should have been born.[25] Only in exceptional cases did the child follow the *origo* of his mother. This, as Ulpian tells us, was by reason of a privilege granted to certain cities.[26]

---

[20] C. X. 40 (39). 7.

[21] E. Cuq, "Origo," *Dictionnaire des Antiquites*, IV, 237.

[22] D. L. 1. 1.

[23] C. X. 40 (39). 7.

[24] D. L. 1. 6. sec. 1; C. X. 39 (38) 3.

[25] J. Brunnemanni, *Commentarius in Codicem Justinianeum*, p. 967; D. L. 1. 1. pr.; C. X. 39. 3; cf. D'Angelo, *Jus Digestorum*, n. 426; Vidal, *Institutiones Iuris Civilis Romani*, n. 66; J. Voet, *Commentarius ad Pandectas*, lib. V, tit. I, n. 91.

[26] D. L. 1. 1. sec. 2.—Savigny, *System*, VIII, §351, *note 1*, says "It is not clear whether the child was a citizen in the native town of the mother alone, or in both places. The latter opinion is in itself more probable."

Illegitimate children followed the *origo* of their mother.[27]

Manumission. Manumission, or liberation from slavery, gave to the freedman, who as a slave possessed no civic rights, the *jus originis* of his patron (former master).[28]

Adoption. By adoption, the person adopted acquired, in addition to his own *origo*, the *jus originis* of his adoptive father.[29]

Adlectio (allectio). Adlectio, or the conferment of citizenship by a community, admitted outsiders to a share in the *jus originis.* This method of acquiring citizenship is first mentioned in the Code, as a constitution of the Emperors Diocletian and Maxiniam.[30] From the fact that the Digests do not refer to it, it does not seem to have existed during the period of classical law.[31] Of the above mentioned ways of acquiring citizenship in a local community, the first, birth or natural descent (*origo, nativitas*) was the usual and most common way.[32] For this reason the expressions *origio* and *jus originis* were used to designate this form of citizenship in general; and the words *originarii* and *originales* to describe all citizens,

---

[27] D. L. 1. 9.

[28] D. L. 1. 6. sec. 3; D. L. 1. 22. sec. 2; D. L. 1. 27; C. X. 39 (38) 2; Aulus Gellius, Apud Festum, *De Verborum significatione,* verbum "Municeps;" Vidal, *l. c.;* Savigny, *System,* VIII, §351: "The acquisition by manumission could, however, be asserted only of a complete manumission. The *dedititii* were not citizens in the municipality of their patron; and the same holds of the *Latini Juniani.*"

[29] D. L. 1. 15. sec. 3.

[30] C. X. 40 (39) 7.

[31] D. L. 1. 1.

[32] Savigny, *l. c.*

not only those who acquired citizenship by birth, but also those who acquired it by the other ways.[33]

§2. *Plurality of Citizens Rights*

Was it possible for an individual to have more than one *origo*? An examination of the texts of the Digests proves that not only was this possible, but that very often such was the case. Thus, Papinian tells us that an adopted person acquires the *jus originis* of his adoptive father, and at the same time retains his own. "*Jus originis in honoribus obeundis ac muneribus suscipiendis adoptione non mutatur, sed novis quoque muneribus filius per adoptivum patrem adstringitur.*"[34] Again, Ulpian tells us that a slave who is freed by many masters acquired the *origo* of everyone of them. "*Si quis a pluribus manumissus sit, omnium patronorum originem sequitur.*"[35] Other cases might be offered, but the above mentioned are sufficient to establish the principle that more than one *jus originis* might be possessed by the same individual.[36]

§3. *Loss of Citizenship*

It was a principle of Roman law that one could not lose or give up his *origo*, either directly, by an act of his will,[37] or indirectly, by a false or erroneous

[33] Savigny, *l. c.;* D'Angelo, *Jus Digestorum,* Vol. I, n. 425; Ferrini, *Pandette,* n. 69.

[34] D. L. 1. 15 sec. 3.

[35] D. L. 1. 7.

[36] E. Cug, "Origo," *Dictionnaire des Antiquites,* IV 237, where the case is cited of a person who obtained the *jus originis* of six local cities by *adlectio;* Bonfante, *Instituzioni di diritto Romano,* n. 17; Ferrini, *Pandette,* n. 69; Declareuil, *Rome the Law Giver,* p. 34.

[37] "Origine propria neminem posse voluntate sua eximi, manifestum est."—C. X. 39 (38). 4.

statement.[38] The good pleasure of the individual citizen was of no avail. The bond by which one was attached to a certain city was determined by law, and it was by law alone that it could be broken.[39] It is in this fact that we note the chief difference between the Roman *origo* and modern "nationality," to which the *origo* has often been compared.[40] Whereas *origo* could not be lost by an act of one's will, one's nationality in our day is lost by the voluntary acceptance of citizenship in another country.

§4. *The Effects of Citizenship*

In the first place the *municeps* was bound by the particular laws of his municipality (*lex originis*).[41] These laws differed in the various cities, and, at times, might prove to be of no small importance. Such, for example, were the laws defining a man's personal capacity in general;[42] laws determining the interpretation of contracts,[43] those establishing the rate of interest [44] and the like. Again, the *municeps* enjoyed the particular privileges (*honores*) of his own city, and at the same time was obliged to share its burdens and obligations (*munera*).[45] In the next place, the *municeps* was subject to the municipal jurisdiction of the city and was bound to submit himself to the

---

[38] D. L. 1. 6. pr.

[39] D. L. 1. 16; J. Cujas, *Opera Omnia*, II, 637; D'Angelo, *Jus Digestorum*, I, n. 425.

[40] Cf. P. Fourneret, *Le Domicile Matrimonial*, pp. 14–15.

[41] Aulus Gellius, *Atticae Noctes*, XVI, 13; Savigny, *System*, VIII, §350

[42] E. A. Whittuck-Poste, *Gai Institutiones Juris Civilis*, p. 297.

[43] D. L. 17. 34.

[44] D. XXII. 1. 37.

[45] D. L. 1. 15 sec. 3; cf. D. L. 4. 1. sec. 1–2 and D. L. 4.18 for the sum total of the *munera*. Cf. Ferrini, *Pandette*, n. 69.

local magistrates.[46] Finally, the inhabitants of towns enjoying the *jus civitatis*, possessed a double citizenship, viz., citizenship at Rome and in the city of their *origo*.[47]

The *origo*, then, considered in itself, was a most important institution of Roman law. It receives, besides an added importance when it is remembered that it gave rise to another institution of Roman law, viz., the domicile, which, since that time, has been and remains today a fundamental part of civil and canonical legislation.[48]

ARTICLE III.—DOMICILE

The laws, privileges and obligations which belonged to those enjoying the *jus originis* of a local municipality, might also be possessed by non-citizens residing in the city. This extension of the *jus originis*, however, was not bestowed freely and indiscriminately upon all residents. A certain essential condition was required. This important condition was that the individual be what the sources call an *incola* of the city.[49]

That an *incola* shared in the rights and obligations possessed by citizens is abundantly proved by examining those texts in the Digests and in the Code, in which the status of the *incola* is likened to that of the *civis*.[50] Thus the Digests tell us "an *incola* must

[46] D. L. 1. 29. Cf. Ferrini, *l. c.*; Bonfante, *Instituzioni di diritto Romano*, n. 17.

[47] Thus Modestinus says: "*Roma Communis nostra patria est.*"—D. L. 1, 33; Declareuil, *o. c.*, p. 54; Savigny, *o. c.*, §352.

[48] R. Phillimore, *The Law of Domicile*, pp. 12, 13; C. P. Sherman, *Roman Law in the Modern World*, II, 32-33.

[49] D. L. 1. Rubric, *Ad Muncipalem, et de Incolis.*

[50] Voet, *Commentarius*, lib. L, tit. I, n. 3.

appear before those magistrates in the place where he is an *incola*, and before those in theplace where he is a citizen; and not only is the *incola* subject to the municipal jurisdiction in both municipalities; he must also perform in both places all public duties."[51] According to Diocletian and Maximian, "notwithstanding the special privilege of some city, it is most certain that one is called to perform civil duties only by reason of *origo* or of domicile."[52] Many other texts might be adduced but the foregoing are sufficiently clear on the point.[53]

The *civis* and the *incola* therefore, in effect, did not differ as far as concerned laws, rights and duties. In regard to these, they were practically on the same footing. They did differ, however, in name and in the manner of acquiring the rights of the city. The *civis* acquired the rights of the city by *origo*, the *incola* by domicile.[54] The sum total of the rights and duties of the *civis* was called the *jus originis*,[55] while the same rights and duties of the *incola* constituted the *jus domicilii*.[56] The importance of ascertaining the Roman law of domicile is evident.

For the sake of clearness, it may be noted here that two kinds of domicile were known to the Roman jurists; (1) the voluntary domicile (*domicilium verum, voluntarium*) and (2) the necessary domicile (*domi-*

---

[51] D. L. 1. 29. Voet, *l. c.*

[52] C. X. 40 (39) 6. Cf. J. Cujas, *Opera Omnia*, II, 638.

[53] D. L. 1. 20; D. L. 1. 22 sec. 2; D. L. 1. 29; D. L. 1. 34; C. X. 39 (38) 1; C. X. 39 (38) 5; C. X. 40 (39) 1; C. X. 40 (39) 3–6.

[54] C. X. 40 (39) 7.

[55] D. L. 1. 15 sec. 3.

[56] P. Fourneret, *Le Domicile Matrimonial*, p. 19.

cilium legale, necessarium).[57] It is to the voluntary domicile that one must turn to discover the general theory of domicile, as the legal domicile was a *res ficta*, i.e., it was determined by positive law, regardless of the will of the individual.[58]

§1. *Voluntary Domicile*

A certain progressive clarity in the expression of the notion of domicile may be noticed by examining, in chronological order, the texts of the Digests and the Code defining it.[59] Alfenus Varus, in the Digests gives us the first definition of domicile: "*Sed de ea re constitutum esse, eam domum unicuique nostrum debere existimari, ubi quisque sedes et tabulas haberet suarumque rerum constitutionem fecerit.*"[60] According to Varus, it is an established principle that domicile is the place where one has settled himself, and has set up in that place his possessions. The jurist Pomponius (ć. 150 A. D.) speaks of those, *qui in oppidi finibus ita agrum habent, ut in eum se quasi in aliquam sedem recipiant.*"[61] Whereas Varus seems to stress material stability, in this fragment of Pom-

---

[57] D. L. 1. 22. sec. 3. Cf. F. Laurin, "Wesen und Bedeutung des Domicils," *Archiv für katholisches Kirchenrecht*, XXVI, 171–2; P. Fourneret, *Le Domicile Matrimonial*, p. 34 ff.; D'Angelo, *Jus Digestorum*, I, n. 427; Voet, *Commentarius*, lib. V. tit. I. n. 93.

[58] B. Windscheid, *Lehrbuch des Pandectenrechts*, vol. I, n. 36; D'Angelo, *l. c.*

[59] According to D'Angelo and Carnelutti, the notion of domicile in Roman law underwent an evolution, brought about by changing social conditions. ". . . (a) initio DOMUS et DOMICILIUM unum idemque juridice significant commorationem; (b) postea DOMICILIUM sumitur ut *commoratio stabilis* in sensu materiali; (c) vi possibilis mobilitatis iudicitur elementum intentionale (C. X. 40. 7.)."

[60] D. L. 16. 203.

[61] D. L. 16. 239 sec. 2.

ponius, though vaguely, the intention of stability is suggested. The last and clearest notion of domicile is that of the Emperors Diocletian and Maximian: "*Et in eo loco, singulos habere domicilium non ambigitur, ubi quis larem rerumque ac fortunarum summam constituit, unde rursus non sit discessurus, si nihil avocet, unde cum profectus est peregrinari videtur: quod si rediit, peregrinari jam destitit.*"[62]

In Roman law, then, domicile means, first of all, the act of dwelling perpetually (*habitatio perpetua*), i.e., the dwelling which a person has begun in a certain place with the intention of remaining there permanently. In this sense the word domicile would be equivalent to the word residing. Besides this, domicile means also the place where a person has begun to dwell with the intention of remaining there permanently. Here the English equivalent would be residence. It is clear that the act of dwelling (the residing) and the dwelling place (residence) are intimately connected, and that the one cannot actually exist without the other. From an examination of the foregoing texts and of others which we shall adduce later, and from what has been said thus far, it is evident that domicile in Roman law was composed of two elements, viz., the intention of permanent residence and actual residence or habitation.[63]

Intention (animus). The intention of permanent residence, so clearly set forth in the second part of

[62] C. X. 40 (39) 7.

[63] Donnellus characterizes the definition of the Emperors as "majore venustatis quam certitudine definitionis", and continues, "Pressius igitur et certius sic domicilium cujusque privatum recte definietur: ut sit locus in quo quis habitat eo animo ut ibi perpetuo consistat nisi quid avocet."—Donnellus, *Comm. in jure civili*, lib. XVIII, c. 12.

the definition of the Emperors, has received at their hands a twofold qualification. In the first place, the intention must not necessarily be absolute and irrevocable, as though one must intend to remain in a place forever. An indefinite stability is all that is required—*si nihil avocet.* A person must intend to remain in the place where he has constituted his domicile if nothing unforeseen happens that would cause his departure. Again, it is not necessary that one remain in the place of domicile at all times. On the contrary, the law makes express mention of occasional departures. When a person has departed in this way, he does not lose his domicile. The law tells us that he is to be regarded as a wanderer, as being away from home; and when he has returned, he is to be regarded as having come back to his home again.[64]

Habitation (*factum*). The "*aliquam sedem*" of which Pomponius speaks,[65] the place "*ubi quis sedes et tabulas haberet*" of Varus,[66] and the "*locus ubi quis larem rerumque fortunarum summam constituit*" of the Emperors,[67] signify nothing other than the central seat of one's affairs, both business and social—his residence or habitation. The foregoing texts indicate also that this residence is not merely a place where one stays for a short time by reason of business or vacation, but that it is something permanent and stable.[68]

---

[64] Cf. H. Dernberg, *System des Römischen Rechts*, n. 38, who cites the example of a merchant who is frequently absent from his home on matters of business.

[65] D. L. 16, 239. sec. 2'

[66] D. L. 16. 203.

[67] C. X. 40 (39). 7.

[68] Cf. D. L. 1. 27. sec. 1.

Constitution of Domicile. When a person begins to dwell in a place with the intention of remaining there permanently, at that moment he acquires a domicile. The intention of permanent residence placed, so to speak, upon the material habitation, changes that simple fact of residence into the juridical being—domicile. Both elements are required. Neither will suffice.

Habitation alone is not sufficient. This is clearly indicated in a fragment of Ulpian, in the Digests, where the great jurist is commenting on the *Lex Cornelia de injuriis.*[69] It seems that Labeo contends that only a person who has a domicile receives the protection afforded by this law.[70] Ulpian, on the contrary, declares that this law pertains to every habitation in which a man may dwell, even though in that place he has not a domicile.[71] The jurist then offers the case of a student. Although the student has not a domicile at his place of studies, nevertheless, if his home is entered by force, he will receive the protection of the Lex Cornelia. Ulpian concludes by saying "*ceterum ad hos pertinebit (lex Cornelia), qui inhabitant non momenti causa, licet ibi domicilium non habeant.*"[72] The conclusion is evident. A man may have a residence or habitation without having a domicile, which would not be true if residence or habitation alone sufficed to constitute a domicile.

The sources explicitly state other elements or acts,

---

[69] D. XLVII. 10. 5. "Lex Cornelia de injuriis competit ei qui injuriarum agere volet ob eam rem, quod se pulsatum, verberatumve domumve suam vi introitam esse dicat."

[70] D. XLVII. 10. 5. sec. 5.

[71] D. XLVII. 10. 5. sec. 5; H. Gasparri, *De Domicilio et Quasi-domicilio*, n. 9.

[72] D. XLVII. 10. 5. sec. 5.

the placing of which do not constitute a domicile. Thus Papinian declares: "The mere possession of a house does not constitute a domicile."[73] The Code declares the same and adds that a domicile is not constituted even if the house or property in question were of the estate of a decurion.[74]

Intention alone does not suffice to constitute a domicile.[75] From the definitions of domicile already examined, particularly the first part of that of the Emperors, it cannot be doubted that habitation is a necessary element in the constitution of a domicile. In fact, this is expressly stated in a text of Paulus; "*Domicilium re et facto transferteur, non nuda contestatione.*"[76]

The opposite opinion, however, has been put forth by some few authors.[77]

In their opinion, residence is not necessary in order to constitute a domicile. According to them "the sole element constitutive of domicile is the act of the will."[78] In support of this contention, some texts of the Digests and the Code are adduced, which do not, however, prove that intention alone constitutes domicile.

The first text, "*Nihil est impedimento quominus quis ubi velit habeat domicilium, quod ei interdictum non sit,*"[79] speaks merely of the freedom everyone enjoyed

---

[73] D. L. 1. 17. sec. 13.

[74] D. X. 40 (39). 4.

[75] Voet, *Commentarius*, lib. V, tit. *I*, n. 98: "Illud certum est, neque solo animo . . . sine re et facto domicilium constitui."

[76] D. L. 1. 20.

[77] P. Fourneret, *Le Domicile Matrimonial*, pp. 27-32; M. J. O'Donnell, "Domicile," *Irish Theological Quarterly*, X, (1915), 132–133.

[78] P. Fourneret, *Le Domicile Matrimonial*, p. 132.

[79] D. L. 1. 31.

to establish his domicile wherever he chose, provided it was not forbidden him; but it says nothing whatsoever of the manner of acquiring a domicile.

The second text is a fragment of Celsus. "*Si quis instructus sit duobus locis aequaliter, neque hic, quam illic minus frequenter commoretur, ubi domicilium habeant, existimatione animi esse accipiendum.*"[80] This text does not prove that residence is not necessary for the constitution of domicile, and that the act of the will alone suffices. The idea conveyed is this: A man has two simple residences of fact. In which has he his domicile? In that to which he has conjoined the intention to remain there permanently In other words, Celsus declares that, of the two places in which a man may have a residence of fact, it is in that place of residence where he intends to remain permanently that he has a domicile.

The third text is an enactment of Diocletian and Maximian contained in the Code.[81] "*Privilegio speciali civitatis non interveniente, tantum originis ratione, ac domicilii voluntate, ad munera civilia quemque vocari certissimum est.*" It is argued that the words *domicilii voluntas* as opposed to *originis ratio* indicate that the act of the will alone is the constitutive element of a domicile. But these words convey merely the idea that a man's *origo* is something he possesses necessarily, while his domicile is acquired voluntarily. It must be admitted that the intention is the dominant factor, but it must also be said that habitation or residence is an essential element in the constitution of a domicile. If intention alone sufficies how explain the statement of Ulpian. "If

[80] D. L. 1. 27. sec. 2.

[81] C. X. 40 (39). 6.

a man always transacts his business not in a colony, but in a city; if he sells, buys and forms contracts there, attends public displays, celebrates festal days, and, in a word enjoys the advantage of city rather than of colonial life, he holds a domicile there, rather than in another place where business affairs may induce him to remain?"[82] In this fragment, Ulpian clearly stresses the material element of domicile. The performance of the various actions, and the enjoyment of the many advantages enumerated in the text, demand a person's residence in the particular city. The evidence is unmistakable.

The authors of the opposing view finally ask the question, if intention alone is not the constitutive element of domicile, how can one explain certain legal domiciles?[83] The domicile of the wife is especially stressed. But this offers no serious difficulty. The legal domicile in Roman law was a *res ficta.* It was constituted by the operation of law, regardless of the intention of the party concerned.[84] The words of the Code are decisive on the point. "We determine," says the Code. "*Mulieres honore maritorum erigimus, et genere nobilitamus, et forum ex eorum persona statuimus.*"[85] The wife did not acquire a domicile of her own. Her intention was unimportant.[86] The law gave to her the domicile of her husband.

---

[82] D. L. 1. 27 sec. 1.

[83] P. Fourneret, *Le Domicile Matrimonial*, p. 32; M. J. O'Donnell, *Domicile,—Irish Theological Quarterly*, X, (1915), 133.

[84] J. Hellfeld, *Jurisprudentia Forensis*, n. 514; B. Windscheid, *Lehrbuch des Pandectenrechts*, vol. I, pp. 89–90; P. Vidal, *Institutiones Juris Civilis*, n. 81; S. D'Angelo, *Jus Digestorum*, t. I, n. 427.

[85] C. X. 40 (39). 9.

[86] B. Windscheid, *Lehrbuch des Pandectenrechts*, vol. 1, pp. 89–90; Cf. S. D'Angelo, *Jus Digestorum*, t. I, p. I, n. 427.

The opinion, then, of those who hold that residence is not a constitutive element of domicile cannot be admitted. In addition to the fact that they have failed to prove their point, it might be added that every other commentator and interpreter of Roman law, consulted on the point, consider both habitation and intention (*factum et animus*) necessary for the constitution of a domicile.[87]

§2. *Legal or Necessary Domicile*

This second kind of domicile was, as has been said above, a *res ficta.* Its acquisition did not depend upon the free choice of the individual. It was, on the contrary, established by law. The law decided where certain persons had a domicile, and by that fact the persons had there a domicile.[88] Thus the married woman had the domicile of her husband.[89] This domicile she retained even after his death, except in the event that she married again. In this case she lost

[87] Accursius, Gloss. on D. L. 1. 20.V. Domicilium "facto, subintellige, et animo; nam haec duo sunt necessaria."; Bartolus, *Opera Omnia*, VI, 218; A. Alciati, *Opera Omnia*, V, 45; H. Donnellus, *Opera Omnia*, IV, 1214; J. Brunnemanni, *Commentarius in Pandectas*, II, 454; Strykius, *Opera Omnia*, vol. XIV, disp. XI, cap. XI, n. 17; M. Sabelli, *Summa Diversorum Tractatuum*, I, 470–471; *Universa Civilis et Criminalis Jurisprudentia*, XII, n. 464; J. Hellfeld, *Jurisprudentia Forensis*, n. 512; B. Windscheid, *Lehrbuch des Pandectenrechts*, I, n. 36; H. Dernberg, *System des Römischen Rechts*, n. 38; F. Laurin, "Wesen und Bedeutung des Domicils," *Archiv für katholisches Kirchenrecht*, XXVI (1871), 166; P. Vidal, *Institutiones Iuris Civilis Romani*, n. 81; C. P. Sherman, *Roman Law in the Modern World*, II, 33; S. D'Angelo, *Jus Digestorum*, T. I, pt. I, n. 427; H. Gasparri, *De Domicilio et Quasi-Domicilio*, n. 8; N. Farren, *Domicile and Quasi-Domicile*, p. 12.

[88] B. Windscheid, *Lehrbuch des Pandectenrechts*, I, 89-90; J. Hellfeld, *Jurisprudentia Forensis*, n. 514; F. Laurin, "Wesen und Bedeutung des Domicils," *Archiv für katholisches Kirchenrecht*, XXVI (1871), 171–2.

[89] C. XII, 1. 13; C. X. 40 (39) 9; D. L. 1. 38 sec. 3; D. XXIII. 2. 5; cf. Ferrini, n. 69.

the domicile of her first husband and acquired that of her second husband.[90] These rules applied only in the condition of lawful marriage (*justae nuptiae*). In an unlawful marriage (*nuptiae non justae*) the woman did not acquire the domicile of her "husband."[91] It might be mentioned here, that the famous *Ea quae* informs us that an engaged woman does not change her domicile before her marriage.[92] Senators possessed a domicile in the city of Rome, even though, by reason of a privilege, they were not bound to residence there.[93] Soldiers had a domicile in their place where they were garrisoned, if they did not have one in their native city.[94] A distinction must be made in the case of exiles. The perpetual exile had a necessary domicile, and that alone, in the place of his exile.[95] The temporary exile, on the other hand, besides acquiring a necessary domicile in the place to which he was banished, retained his voluntary domicile.[96]

§3. *Domicile of Children* (*Filiifamilias*)

In Roman law it is quite clear that children (*filiifamilias*) were free to choose their own domicile. This fact is explicitly stated in two fragments of Ulpian contained in the Digests.[97] The freedom

[90] D. L. 1. 22. sec. 1; C. X. 40 (39) 9.

[91] D. L. 1. 37. sec. 2.

[92] D. L. 1. 32.

[93] D. L. 1. 22. sec. 6.

[94] D. L. 1. 23. sec. 1; cf. Ferrini, *Pandette*, n. 69.

[95] D. L. 1. 22. sec. 3; cf. Ferrini, *l. c.*

[96] D. L. 1. 27. sec. 3. Cf. also Robert Phillimore, *The Law of Domicile*, pp. 62–63; B. Windscheid, *Lehrbuch des Pandectenrechts*, vol. I, p. 90.

[97] D. L. 1. 3. 4. "Placet etiam, filiusfamilias domicilium habere posse; non utique ibi, ubi pater habuit, sed ubicumque ipse domicilium constituit. D. L. 1. 6. 1: "Filius civitatem ex qua pater ejus naturalem originem ducit, domicilium non sequitur.

of children to choose a domicile distinct from that of the father was admitted also by the Glossa,[98] and by the Commentators generally.[99] The testimony of the Glossa is very valuable since, according to Riccobono,[100] the Glossa reflects in great part the pure Justinian law.

It is to be noted that some commentators, while admitting the freedom of children to choose their domicile, were wont to make two observations: (1) Unless the opposite were certain, the presumption was that the child retained the domicile of the father.[101] (2) The right to constitute a domicile was restricted to those who had attained the age of puberty, since, before that time, a child did not have the *animus* essential to the constitution of domicile.[102]

§4. *Domicile of Students*

In early Roman law, according to a fragment of Ulpian,[103] the residence of a student in a University City was not held to confer a domicile, no matter how long he continued to reside there. His residence in the place of his studies was looked upon as special and temporary, and therefore, the intention to remain indefinitely, one of the essential elements of domicile, did not, in his case, exist. This law was

---

[98] Gloss on D. L. 1. 6. v. *non domicilium*: "cum ipse filius sua voluntate sibi constituit ubi vult

[99] Bartolus in D. L. 1. 3. "Filiusfamilias potest sibi constituere domicilium. "Cujas in lib. 1 Responsa Papin: "Coeli et domicilii libera cuique est, patrifamilias vel filiofamilias." Cf. Voet, in Pandectas, lib. V, tit, 1, n. 100.

[100] Riccobono, "Stipulatio ed instrumentum nel Diritto giustinianeo," *Zeitschrift der Savigny-Stiftung*, 43, 388–89.

[101] *Universa Civilis et Criminalis Jurisprudentia*, lib. IV. 475.

[102] Huberi, *Prael. Juris Civilis*, vol. II, lib. V, tit. 1, n. 45.

[103] D. XLVII. 10. 5. sec. 5.

relaxed somewhat by a decree of the Emperor Hadrian. In this decree, Hadrian specified that if students resided in the place of studies for a period of ten years, they were considered to have there a domicile—"*domicilium ibi habere creduntur.*"[104] Is Hadrian, in this passage, making an exception to the general rule, or is he merely stating a presumption? From the words of the decree—*habere creduntur*—it seems evident that he is merely stating a presumption. Therefore, if the student de facto had no intention of permanently residing in the place of studies, even though he remained there for ten years, he did not acquire there a domicile. This interpretation has the advantage that it safeguards the general principles of domicile, which proclaim the absolute necessity of the *animus permanendi.* At the same time, it has the support of many authorities, including the eminent jurists, Cujas and Bartolus.[105]

It may be mentioned here that this question is not without some historical importance. In the first place, the presumption of the existence of a domicile from the fact of ten years residence, applicable only to students in Roman law, was extended to include all cases by the jurists of the school of Bologna.[106] And curiously enough, in the second place, the ten years residence has found a not insignificant position in the Code of Canon Law where it exists, not merely as a presumption, but as a lone constitutive of domicile.[107]

---

[104] C. X. 40 (39) 2.

[105] Bartolus, *Opera Omnia,* vol. VIII, p. 21; J. Cujas, *Opera Omnia,* vol. II, c. 638; Mascardus, *De Probationibus,* vol. I, Concl. DXXXV, n. 13 ff.; F. Wharton, *Conflict of Laws,* p. 8; Savigny, *System,* VIII, §353.

[106] Accursius, Gloss on *Constituerint* C. X. 40 (39) 2.

[107] Canon 92, § 1.

§5. *Plurality of Domiciles*

It was a recognized principle of Roman law that a man might possess more than one domicile.[108] We shall let the Roman jurists speak for themselves.

Ulpian relates that "it is the opinion of prudent men that an individual could possess a domicile in two places, if he so arranged matters, that he seemed to have established himself in one place no less than in the other."[109]

In another text Ulpian states the same fact. "It is true," he says, "that a person can have a domicile in two places, but it is something difficult."[110]

Paulus informs us that Labeo contends that a person who establishes himself in many places has no domicile. Labeo, however, refers to the fact that many other jurists declare that a person can have a domicile in many places. This latter opinion, Paulus states, is the truer.[111]

A text of Paulus, taken in conjunction with one of Ulpian, also proves that a man may have more than one domicile, although in this case, one of the domiciles is a legal or necessary domicile. Paulus declares that an exile has a necessary domicile in the place in which he is exiled, and according to Ulpian, an exile can have a domicile in the place from which he has been exiled.[112]

---

[108] Ferrini, *Pandette*, n. 60; D'Angelo, *Jus Digestorum*, I, n. 427.

[109] D. L. 1. 6. sec. 2.

[110] D. L. 1. 27. sec. 2.

[111] D. L. 1. 5. Cf. also Cujas, *Opera Omnia*, vol. IV, c. 592 and vol. V, c. 619–620.

[112] D. L. 1. 22. sec. 3. D. L. 1. 27. sec. 3.

§6. *Lack of Domicile*

Could a person be without a domicile? It seems that a person could be without a domicile, although this condition of affairs was regarded as rare in Roman law. Ulpian, after stating that it was difficult to have many domiciles, adds "just as it is difficult for one to be without a domicile." "But," he continues, "I think that this can happen if a person, having abandoned his domicile, goes on a sea voyage, or journeys on land, seeking a place to which he can betake himself and here become established, for I regard this man as being without a domicile."[113]

§7. *Loss of Domicile*

Domicile, unlike *origo*, could be lost or transferred. A domicile, in Roman law, was lost in the same way in which it was acquired, i.e., by the intention of departing and not returning, and by actual departure. "*Domicilium*," says Paulus, "*re et facto transfertur, non nuda contestatione*."[114]

§8. *Place of Domicile*

Although one frequently finds the phrase "*domicilium in provincia*" mentioned in the sources, it seems to be the generally accepted opinion that the place of domicile, whether voluntary or necessary, was the city or municipality (*civitas, municipium*).[115] When one considers that the domicile was an extension of the

---

[113] D. L. 1. 27. sec. 2. Cf. D'Angelo, *l. c.*; Ferrini, *Pandette* n. 69.

[114] D. L. 1. 20.

[115] Cf. P. Fourneret, *Le Domicile Matrimonial*, pp. 47–59; cf. also N. Farren, *Domicile and Quasi-domicile*, pp. 15–16; F. X. Wernz, Votum —*Analecta Ecclesiastica*, 7 (1899), 66, n. 13; P. Gasparri, *De Matrimonio*, II, n. 941.

origo, and that the *origo* was confined in its operation to the city or municipality, it is difficult to escape the conclusion that the local city was the place of domicile, and that the provincial domicile as such was, at least, not a general principle of Roman law. We think, however, that in certain extraordinary circumstances a person might have a provincial domicile as such. We do not intend to labor the point, but merely offer the following passage of a commentator on the Digests of Justinian, and leave it to the reader to judge its value. "*Praeterea sunt in quaque Rep. vel provincia plures, qui ratione domicilii indigenae magis Reipubl. provinciaeve, quam certi loci in quo commorantur, esse videntur, quales sine dubio sunt, qui nusquam certa sede, quod appareat, ac habitatione conquiescunt, ut sub quo judice convenire debeant, ignoretur. Hos ad supremam curiam sive Praesidem vocari posse, atque debere, manifestum est, sive alicubi deprehendantur, sive per edictum citandi sint.*"[116]

§9. *Effects of Domicile*

"Domicile," says the Code, "makes one an *incola*."[117] And the *incola*, we have already seen, was practically on the same legal footing as the *municeps* (*civis*).[118] Thus the *incola* was bound by the law of the municipality in which he had a domicile; he enjoyed there the *jus domicilii*, embracing both privileges and burdens, and was subject to the municipal magistrates and jurisdiction.[119]

---

[116] Ulr. Huberi, *Praelectionum Juris Civilis*, vol. II, p. 236.

[117] C. X. 40 (39) 7.

[118] Cf. above p 11.

[119] Cf. above p 11.; Pauly-Wissowa, *Real Encyclopedie der Classischen Altertumswissenschaft*, V, 1299–1300; D'Angelo, *Jus Digestorum*, I, n. 427.

§10. *Domicile and Origo*

From what has been said, it is evident that in Roman law the terms *origo* and *domicilium* conveyed two entirely distinct notions. The *origo* and the domicile, it is true, agreed in this, that they were means of subjecting individuals to the jurisdiction, laws and burdens of a place.[120] Yet there were many differences between them. In the first place, while the *civis* was attached to a community, independently of his own free choice, as if from a certain necessity, i.e., by reason of birth,[121] the *incola* became attached to a certain city by his own free will, i.e., by the voluntary constitution of a domicile.[122] Again, the *civis* was subject to the laws and jurisdiction of his municipality, whether he willed it or not; nor could he, by migrating to another city, release himself from the obligations of his city of origin.[123] On the other hand, the *incola*, as by his own free choice he became subject to the laws and jurisdiction of a certain city, so also could he, by exercising another free choice, liberate himself from these obligations, by moving to another city.[124] It is clear, then, that there was an essential difference between the *civis* and the *incola*, between the *jus originis* and the *jus domicilii.*

§11. *Conclusion*

Such was the Roman law of domicile. Its importance cannot be over-emphasized. Side by side with

[120] D. L. 1. 29. C. X. 40 (39) 6. Cf. p. 11.

[121] D. L. 1. 6. pr. Cf. Savigny, *System*, VIII, §353.

[122] C. X. 40 (39) 6. Cf. Savigny, *l. c.*

[123] C. X. 39 (38) 4; D. L. 1. 16. Cf. D'Angelo, *o. c.*, n. 425.

[124] D. L. 1. 31; cf. Savigny, *System*, VIII, §353; D'Angelo, *Jus Digestorum*, I, n. 425.

the *origo*, it played a leading part in the municipal life of the Empire, and whereas the *origo*, as it existed in Roman law, has since disappeared, the domicile, its legal descendant, has achieved a position of great prominence in subsequent legal history, stretching its tentacles over numerous portions of civil and canon law. It is true that, for a time, the principles of domicile, though not entirely forgotten, had little influence in the subjection of the individual to a particular forum. This fact was due, authorities tell us, to the general disorder resulting from the barbarian invasions.[125] In the barbarian codes it was no longer domicile, but merely habitation and race that determined the legal status of individuals during these times.[126] The Justinian Code, however, outlived those of the barbarians, and with the foundation of the school of Bologna, interest was revived in the study of Roman law. The Bolognese jurists expounded, in the main, the general principles of Justinian law, but on some few points their teachings marked a departure from what we know of Roman law. For example, their notion of the *origo* was quite different from the true Roman notion. According to them, the *origo* was a species of domicile, the *domicilium originis*.[127] Again, as has been stated above, the presumption of domicile from ten years

---

[125] A. Boudinhon, "Domicile," *Catholic Encyclopedia*, V. 104; N. Farren, *Domicile and Quasi-domicile*, p. 16.

[126] M. J. O'Donnell, "Domicile," *Irish Theological Quarterly*, X (1915), 137; N. Farren, *Domicile and Quasi-domicile*, p. 17; M. Ortolan, *History of Roman Law*, p. 432.

[127] Accursius, Gloss on D. L. 1. 6; M. J. O'Donnell, "Domicile," *Irish Theological Quarterly*, X (1915), p. 138.

residence, made originally in favor of students, was extended to all classes. A final point, worthy of mention, is the fact that these jurists, rightly in our estimation, stressed the importance of the material element in the constitution of domicile.[128]

---

[128] Accursius, Gloss on C. X. 40 (39) 7; A. Boudinhon, "Domicile," *Catholic Encyclopedia*, V. 104.

CHAPTER II

DOMICILE IN CANON LAW

In tracing the development of domicile in canon law three periods may be distinguished: from the beginning to the Decree of Gratian (c. 1140); from the Decree of Gratian to the Council of Trent (1545-1563); from the Council of Trent to the publication of the Code of Canon Law.

Article I.—From the Beginning to the Decree of Gratian

The domicile, as we have seen, was an important and useful institution in Roman Law. Its importance and utility could not but recommend it to the early canonists and ecclesiastical authorities. Yet important and useful as it had been to the Roman jurists, and could have been to the canonists, the fact remains that prior to the time of Gratian, domicile was an entirely unknown institution in canon law. In fact, the word itself is never even mentioned either in the early collections of ecclesiastical laws or in the decrees of Councils. In a word, ancient canon law had no theory of domicile, nor did domicile regulate the general exercise of local jurisdiction.

A brief examination of the writings of canonists and the decrees of Councils in regard to the reception of the sacraments, judicial competence, the payment of tithes and ecclesiastical burial, questions about which domicile, if it existed during this period, should have been concerned, will establish the fact that domicile had no part in the disciplinary code of the early church.

1. In regard to the sacraments, the question of the proper bishop for the reception of the sacrament of Orders alone shall be considered, since that has ever proved to be a fruitful field for domiciliary legislation.[1] Two classes of persons are to be distinguished: laymen and clerics. In regard to laymen, the council of Sardis (343) decreed that no bishop should ordain a layman of another bishop (i.e., bishop of origin).[2] This discipline was confirmed at a synod held in Carthage (348), at which Gratus, the Primate of Carthage, was present.[3] From that time, however, until the ninth century the decrees of Popes and the canons of councils are silent concerning the ordination of laymen. This silence and the example of many laymen, among them Jerome and Augustine, who were ordained by bishops other than their own, without any question being raised regarding the necessity of the latter's consent, have led Thomassin to conclude that during that time bishops were free to ordain laymen of another bishop.[4]

A change in this discipline was inaugurated by the council of Mayence in 888,[5] and repeated in the councils of Ravenna in 997[6] and of London in 1125.[7] The tenth canon of the council of London gives the

[1] It was not until the publication of the decree "*Tametsi*" that domicile entered into the question of marriage.

[2] Canon XVIII—Mansi, III, 29.

[3] Canon V—Mansi, III, 147.

[4] L. Thomassin, *Vetus et Nova Ecclesiae Disciplina*, pt. II, c. 1–5.

[5] Canon XIV—Mansi, XVIII A, 68.

[6] Canon III—Mansi, vol. XIX, col. 220.

[7] Canon X—Mansi, vol. XXI, col. 332.

substance of the new discipline: "*Nullus episcopus alterius praesumat parochianum ordinare.*"[8] The councils do not relate what constitutes a parishioner, or what subjects him to a certain bishop for ordination. According to Thomassin, it is the bishop of origin.[9]

The law in regard to clerics was quite different. The canons and decrees of councils throughout the whole period, beginning with the council of Nicea in 325, are absolute in their prohibition of bishops to retain or promote to a higher order the cleric of another bishop. In the words of the Council of London (1075): "*Ex multis Romanorum praesulum decretis diversisque sacrorum canonum auctoritatibus, neq uis alienum clericum, vel monachum, sine commendatitiis literis retineat vel ordinet.*"[10]

As in the case of laymen, the councils do not state what constituted one a cleric of another. According to Thomassin and others, the bishop who first ordained a person a cleric was his proper bishop.[11] Previous ordination then was the tie that bound and subjected clerics to their bishops.

Coming finally to the Decree of Gratian, one finds no mention of domicile as a means of obtaining a proper bishop. It was the professed intention of Gratian to give the latest canonical teaching on matters of ecclesiastical importance. Besides this, Gratian was not unaware of the institution of domicile.[12] Yet not once does Gratian speak of domicile

[8] Canon X—Mansi, vol. XXI, col. 332.

[9] Thomassin, *Vetus et Nova Ecclesiae Disciplina*, pt. II, c. VII, n. II.

[10] Mansi, vol. XX, col. 451.

[11] L. Thomassin, *o. c.*, pt. I, c. 1, n. 6; P. Fourneret, *Le Domicile Matrimonial*, pp. 81–82.

[12] Gratian mentions it a few times in regard to other matters. Cf. c. 1, C. XIII, q. 1; c. 6, C. XIII, q. 2.

in regard to the proper bishop of ordination. The conclusion is that during this period candidates for the reception of orders became a bishop's subjects by birth or previous ordination, not by domicile.[13]

2. The principles regarding judicial competence during this period are scant and indefinite. A canon of the Capitulary of Charlemagne declares that no bishop should presume to judge the parishioner of another, and that no one is bound by the sentence of a judge other than his own.[14] A council of London in 1125 echoed this teaching: "*Nullus episcopus alterius praesumat parochianum . . . judicare; unus quisque enim suo domino stat aut cadit; nec tenetur aliquis sententia non a suo judice prolata.*"[15]

In the Decree of Gratian the general principle is stated: "Actor sequitur forum rei."[16] Two canons, elaborating this principle, declare in substance, that in contentious matters in which a lay person is the defendant, he must appear before the judge of his province; in actions in which a cleric is the defendant, the case must be brought to the court of the bishop.[17] One may conclude from these instances that residence of some sort had something to do with the selection of the competent judge. One may also conclude that domicile, as we know it, had no part in that selection.

3. In the early ages of the church no special provision was made for the support of the clergy. The

---

[13] Boniface VIII was the first to attach importance to the domicile as a means of obtaining a proper bishop for ordination. Cf. c. 3, *De temporibus ordinationum*, I, 9, in VI°.

[14] *Capitularium Caroli Magni*, lib. VII, c. 308—Mansi, XVII, 1093

[15] Canon X—Mansi, XXI, 332.

[16] C. 15, C. XI, q. 1.

[17] C. 15, 16, C. XI, q. 1.

faithful, following the example of the Jews, who gave tithes for the support of the levites, provided for the bodily needs of the clergy in return for the spiritual benefits received through their ministry. The payment of tithes, however, was made obligatory by the council of Macon in 585 [18] and insisted upon by many councils thereafter.[19] These councils, however, determined nothing beyond the existence of the obligation, and disputes soon arose as to who was to receive the tithes. To settle this difficulty the council of Chalon sur Saone, in 813, determined the following rule: "*Familiae vere ibi dent decimas suas ubi infantes eorum baptizantur, et ubi per totum anni circulum missas audiunt*"[20] Soon afterwards the council of Pavia, in 855, declared that it was "contrary to the divine law and to the sacred canons that lay people refuse to pay their tithes to the churches where they receive the sacraments and hear the word of God."[21] It can hardly be doubted that the hearing of Mass the year round and the reception of the sacraments in a certain church, which determined the obligation to pay tithes, demanded residence of some permanency. The authorities were struggling in the proper direction, and hence, turning to that part of the Decree of Gratian which treats of tithes, it is not surprising to find there the word domicile mentioned for the first time in canonical history.[22] It is a mere mention, to be sure, unsupported in its use by any of the texts cited, but it is mentioned, and that in an intelligent manner.

[18] Canon V—Mansi, IX, col. 951–2.
[19] Cf. F. X. Funk, *A Manual of Church History*, I, 286.
[20] Canon XIX—Mansi, XIV, 97.
[21] Mansi, XV, 18.
[22] C. 1, C. XIII, q. 1.

4. The word domicile is mentioned for the second time in the Decree in connection with ecclesiastical burial. Gratian reproduces a canon of the Council of Tribur (895) which states that, if for some reason a person cannot be buried in the Cathedral church or in a religious church which he had chosen, then "*ubi quis decimas persolvebat vivus, ibi sepeliatur mortuus.*"[23] Gratian repeats these last words in his commentary on the canon and continues, "*Item si quis de provincia ad provinciam transiret et ibi domicilium sibi collocaret, liber factus a ditione prioris judicis, jurisdictioni illius judicis, subiceretur, in cujus provincia sedem sibi eligeret.*"[24]

To Gratian, therefore, goes the twofold distinction of being the first canonist to mention domicile, and of being the first to attach to it its fundamental function in Roman law, viz., subjection to local jurisdiction. The silence of centuries was broken.

Article II.—From the Decree of Gratian to the Council of Trent

The period from the Decree of Gratian to the Council of Trent is marked by the increasing importance of domicile in matters of ecclesiastical discipline and by the definitive acceptance of the Roman theory by the canonists of the period.

It was in the Decretals themselves that domicile received official recognition as an ecclesiastical institution. Thus in the Decretals of Gregory IX, it was domicile that determined one's proper forum and competent judge.[25] In the famous canon "*cum*

[23] Canon XV—Mansi, XVIII, 140.

[24] C. 6, C. XIII, q. 2.

[25] C. 20, X, *de foro competente*, II, 2.

nullus" in the Liber Sextus of Boniface VIII, the bishop of domicile became the "proprius episcopus" for the conferring of the sacrament of Orders.[26] Finally, another canon of the Liber Sextus decreed that the canonical portion must be paid to the church to which one was attached by domicile.[27]

However, no theory or definition of domicile is contained in the Decretals. One must have recourse to the writings of the Glossators and Commentators on Decretal law to discover the notion and extent of domicile as it was received into canon law.

It is an irrefutable fact that the canonists did not construct a peculiar theory of domicile, but that they accepted and utilized the Roman theory, at least in substance. Authorities are entirely in agreement on this point, and their contention is substantiated by the fact that the canonists, when treating of domicile in their glosses and commentaries on the Decretals, always allege the authority of the pertinent texts of the Digest and the Code of Justinian, or the writings of the Bolognese jurists.[28] This adoption of the Roman law on domicile is not surprising. As one author well states: "The connection between civil and canonical law was too close in those days, and domicile played too great a part in the former not to receive soon some recognition in the latter."[29]

The jurists of Bologna, as noted above,[30] departed

[26] C. 3, *de temporibus ordinationum*, I, 9, in VI°.

[27] C. 2, *de sepulturis*, III, 12, in VI°.

[28] F. Laurin "Wesen und Bedeutung des Domicile," *Archiv für katholisches Kirchenrecht*, XXVI, (1871), 184 ff.: F. X. Wernz,—*Analecta Ecclesiastica*, vol. VII, p. 66: A. Boudinhon, "Domicile," *Catholic Encyclopedia*, V, 104.

[29] H. A. Ayrinhac, *General Legislation in the New Code of Canon Law*, p. 195.

[30] p. 27.

in some instances from a pure Roman notion of domicile, and since they influenced to no small degree a number of the canonists of the period, it is important to give at least a brief sketch of their theory before examining the writings of the canonists.

§1. *The Civil Jurists of Bologna*

The civil jurists of the school of Bologna, which was founded by Irnerius about 1120, were chiefly concerned in writing glosses and commentaries on the Roman law. They are generally classified into three ages or schools: the Glossarists (1100-1260), the Scribentes (1260-1510), and the Humanists (1500-——).[31] As it would be practically impossible to review the teachings of all the jurists of these schools, we shall content ourselves with examining the writings of the recognized leaders of each school.

It is to Accursius, the founder of the school of the Glossarists that we are indebted for several departures from the old Roman law, among them the so-called domicile of origin, and the extension of the presumption of the ten years' residence rule to all classes.[32] Accursius, seems to have entirely misunderstood the Roman *origo*. Whereas in Roman law *origo* signified the legal bond attaching one to a *certain city*, and at the same time signified the *jus originis*, or sum of citizen rights in a certain city, to Accursius, *origo* was the place of birth, whether personal or paternal.[33] In Roman law, too, *origo* was the legal antecedent of domicile, which was introduced at a later date by the Roman jurists to supply a practical

---

[31] M. Ortolan, *History of Roman Law*, p. 541.

[32] M. Ortolan, *o. c.*, p. 543.

[33] Gloss on *nativitas*, D. L. 1. 1.

need.[34] In the mind of Accursius, on the contrary, it would seem that domicile was the dominant idea, the genus of which there were two species, the *domicilium originis*, possessed by those born in a certain place, and the *domicilium habitationis*, possessed by those permanently residing in a place. In a word, Accursius sponsored and established an institution entirely unknown in Roman law, a distortion of the Roman *origo*, the domicile of origin.[35] The determination of the place of the domicile of origin caused a further departure from the Roman law. In the ordinary case, according to Accursius, the son acquired the domicile of origin in the place where his father had his domicile of habitation. In the case, however, of a son born in some place other than where the father was residing, the domicile of origin was acquired, not in the place where the father had his domicile of fact, but where he had his domicile of origin—his actual birthplace.[36]

Error and absurdity followed this conception of Accursius. As a result of this principle, the words *incola* and *civis*, two fundamentally different concepts in Justinian's time, express, to Accursius, quite the same thing. They differed *apparently* in this: a *civis* was one who acquired a domicile by birth, an *incola* one who acquired a domicile by permanent residence.[37] Again, the Roman jurists had stated that a man could be without a domicile. This was a bit difficult for Accursius to understand. A man had to be born somewhere, and did not the Roman law give

---

[34] Cf. p. 10

[35] Gloss on *Domicilio*, D. L. 1. 27. 2.

[36] Gloss on D. L. 1. 6. C. X. 39 (38) 3.

[37] Gloss on D. L. 1. 29.

him a domicile in the place of birth? The solution of Accursius was that the place of birth must have been destroyed by an earthquake, or captured as was the city of Troy.[38] The thing was fanciful and extravagant, but Accursius must be logical.

The second departure of Accursius from the old Roman law was in regard to the ten years residence. As stated above,[39] an enactment of the Emperor Hadrian had decreed that students, who resided in a university town for ten years, were presumed to have there a domicile. In his gloss on the word *constituerint*, Accursius, after referring to this presumption made in favor of students, adds, "*Quid de alio, qui stat per decem annos non causa studii? Respondeo; idem, ut praesumatur domicilium animo constitutum.*"[40]

The teaching of Bartolus, the chief of the second school, the Scribentes, on the domicile of origin cannot be ascertained with certainty. In one passage he seems to depart from the teaching of Accursius.[41] In another, one feels certain he is speaking about the domicile of origin.[42]

In regard to the ten years residence rule, Bartolus refers to the presumption established in favor of students, but says nothing beyond insisting that it is a presumption merely.[43]

Cujas, the glory of the civilians, of whom it is said that "he found the civil law of wood and left it of marble," is the leader of the third school, the Human-

[38] Gloss on *Domicilio*. D. L. 1. 27. 2.

[39] Cf. p. 21.

[40] Gloss on C. X. 40 (39). 2. Cf. Gloss on D. L. 1. 27. 3.

[41] Bartolus, Comm. on D. L. 1. 27. 2.

[42] Bartolus, Comm. on C. X. 39 (38) 2.

[43] Bartolus, Comm. on C. X. 40 (39) 2.

ists. Cujas is a pure Romanist on the question of domicile. The distinction between domicile and *origo* was, in his mind, a clear one. "*Aliud est domicilium, aliud est origo.*"[44] The *incola* and *municeps* (*civis*) were persons quite distinct. "*A municipibus separantur incolae, qui domicilii jure municipii commodis et praecipuis fruuntur.*"[45] Can a person be without a domicile? Certainly, says Cujas. "*Ut autem quis plurium civitatum potest esse municeps, ita et incola: ut sine civitate . . . ita et sine domicilio.*"[46] Unfortunately, however, or fortunately, as one cares to view it, before Cujás wrote his admirable commentaries on Roman law, the teachings of Accursius had already been accepted by almost all the canonists of the period.

§2. *The Glossators and Commentators on the Decretals*

The canonists of this period, as the civil jurists before them, were chiefly concerned in writing glosses and commentaries on the existing codes of law, and it is in these glosses and commentaries that one will discover the notion and scope of domicile as the canonists applied it to canon law.

A. The Glossators. The Gloss of Bartholomew of Brescia (c. 1236) [47] on the Decree of Gratian accepted the theory of Accursius in regard to the ten years' residence rule,[48] and indicated that the bishop of the place where one had a domicile was the proper bishop

[44] J. Cujas, *Opera Omnia*, vol. III, col. 660.

[45] *Op. cit.* vol. II, col. 639.

[46] *Op. cit.*, vol. II, col. 639.

[47] This gloss is really a revision and completion of the Ordinary gloss on the Decree composed by Joannes Teutonicus.

[48] Gloss on *Liber Factus*, C. 6. C. XIII, q. 2.

for the reception of the Sacrament of Orders.[49] The Gloss offers little else of importance in regard to domicile.

There is nothing in the Gloss of Bernard of Parma (c. 1263), the ordinary gloss on the Decretals of Gregory IX, that betrays the influence of the jurists of Bologna. The domicile of origin and the ten years' residence rule were entirely disregarded by Bernard.

It seems that Bernard was more concerned about the application of domicile than about its notion. Only two considerations in regard to the latter are advanced. The mere possession of a house does not constitute a domicile unless it is one "*in qua interdum consueverat habitare.*"[50] Again, a person can have a domicile in many places provided he establish himself equally in *each place.*[51]

Regarding the application of domicile, according to Bernard, domicile made one a parishioner in a determined parish,[52] and subjected him to the jurisdiction of a certain area.[53] Domicile determined one's proper forum and competent judge,[54] and by it also one acquired his proper bishop for the reception of orders.[55]

To Joannes Andreas, the author of the ordinary gloss on the Liber Sextus of Boniface VIII, goes the distinction of having introduced the Bolognese theory of the domicile of origin into canon law.[56] The

---

[49] Gloss on *Obtineat.* C. 6. D. LXXI.

[50] Gloss on *Andegavensi,* c. 15, X, *de foro competente,* II, 2.

[51] Gloss on *Domicilium,* c. 29, X, *de rescriptis,* I, 3. Gloss on *Domicilii,* C. 20, X, *de foro competente,* II, 2.

[52] Gloss on *Si alterius,* c. 2, X, *de parochiis,* III, 29.

[53] Gloss on *Habitatores jurisdictionem,* C. 5, X, *de parochiis,* III, 29.

[54] Gloss on *Aut domicilii,* c. 20, X, *de foro competente,* II, 2.

[55] Gloss on *Praesumat,* c. 3, X, *de parochiis,* III, 29.

[56] Gloss on *Oriundus,* c. 3, *de temporibus ordinationum,* I, 9, in VI°.

influence of the civil jurists of Bologna is also apparent in his acceptance of the universal application of the presumption of the ten years residence rule.[57] A man can have many domiciles and a man can be without a domicile.[58] In this latter case Andreas does not repeat the absurdity of Accursius, but cites the example of the traveler as related by Ulpian in the Digests.[59]

Zenzelius de Cassanis, (1343) who wrote a gloss on the Extravagantes of John XXII, also acknowledged the domicile of origin.[60] This acceptance of the theory of Accursius, and the declaration that a person can have many domiciles [61] constitute his contribution to the history of the canonical domicile.

B. The Commentators. The history of the notion of domicile as found in the writings of the glossators practically repeats itself in the writings of the commentators of the period.

Hostiensis (c. 1271), the first of the commentators to engage our attention, reveals the unmistakable influence of the jurists of Bologna in his adoption of their theory regarding the ten years' residence rule.[62] To the same canonist we are indebted for a complete definition of domicile. It is taken substantially from the Roman law, and is a union of the definition of the

---

[57] Gloss on *Is qui*, c. 3, *de sepulturis*, III, 12, in VI°.

[58] Gloss on *Domicilia*, c. 2, *de sepulturis*, III, 12, in VI°.

[59] D. L. 1. 27. 2.

[60] Gloss on *Commorantur*, c. un., *de praebendis et dignitatibus*, tit. III, in Extravag. Joannis XXII.

[61] Gloss on *Vagandi Materia*, c. un., *de praebendis et dignitatibus*, tit. III, in Extravag. Joannis XXII.

[62] Hostiensis, *Commentarium in tertium librum Decretalium*, c. 20, *de decimis*.

Emperors and that of Ulpian.[63] "*Intelligitur ibi habere domicilium, ubi larem tenet et majorem partem fortunarum suarum et ubi vendit, ubi emit, ubi dies festos colit, et si ab hac discedat peregrinari videtur, et cum redierit peregrinari desiit.*"[64] In another place Hostiensis adds, "*vel etiamsi nihil ibi habeat, dum tamen ibidem continue conversetur.*"[65] A person without a domicile is called a *viator*.[66]

Durandus (c. 1296) has very little on the subject of domicile. It may be for this reason that he repeats none of the errors of the predecessors. Durandus mentions that domicile is a means of obtaining a proper forum and competent judge, gives in substance the definition of the Emperors, and recognizes the fact that a person can be without domicile.[67] *Vagabundus* is the name Durandus uses to designate the latter.[68]

The next and perhaps the greatest canonist of the period is the Abbas Panormitanus (Nicola de Tudeschi, c. 1453) who wrote his commentaries on the Decretals about one hundred years before the Council of Trent. Panormitanus renewed the errors of Accursius, accepting in their entirety his notions of the domicile of origin,[69] and the ten years' residence rule.[70] With these two exceptions the theory pro-

---

[63] C. X. 40 (39) 7; D. L. 1, 27. 1.

[64] Hostiensis, *Commentarium in primum librum Decretalium*, c. 29, *de rescrip.*

[65] Hostiensis, *Commentarium in secundum librum Decretalium*, c. 15, *de foro comp.*

[66] Hostiensis, *Comm. in tertium librum Decretalium*, c. 10, *de sepult.*

[67] Durandus, *Speculum Juris*, lib. I, p. II, n. 30.

[68] Durandus, *l. c.*

[69] Panormitanus, *Comm. in Decretal.*, lib. II, tit. II, C. XIV, n. 4.

[70] *Ibidem.*

pounded by Panormitanus is the theory contained in Roman law. According to Panormitanus, a domicile was acquired when one came to reside in a place with the intention of residing there permanently.[71] It was possible for a person to have many domiciles.[72] One could be without a domicile.[73] As an example of the necessary domicile, Panormitanus declared that the married woman acquired the domicile of her husband.[74] In regard to the effects of domicile in Canon Law, Panormitanus stated that the domicile determined one's proper forum [75] and parochial church,[76] and subjected one to the local jurisdiction.[77]

The last three great canonists who wrote before Trent were Felinus Sandaeus, Bertachinus and Sylvester Prieras.

Felinus wrote at length concerning the domicile of the cleric. According to this writer, a secular cleric who had a benefice requiring residence was commonly thought to have a domicile in the place in which the benefice was situated.[78] If, on the other hand, the cleric had a benefice which did not require residence, he was not considered to have a domicile in the place of his benefice.[79]

Bertachinus and Sylvester bear witness to the fact that, when they wrote, the domicile had an established

---

[71] *Comm. in Decret.*, lib. III, tit, XXIX, C. V, n. 8.
[72] *Comm. in Decret.*, lib. II, tit. II, C. 14, n. 4.
[73] *Comm. in Decret.*, lib. II, tit. II, C. 20, n. 13.
[74] *Comm. in Decret.*, 1. c., n. 30.
[75] *Comm. in Decret.*, 1. c., n. 2.
[76] *Comm. in Decret.*, lib. III, tit. XXVIII, C. 10, n. 10.
[77] *Comm. in Decret.*, lib. III, tit. XXIX, C. 5, n. 4.
[78] Felinus, in c. dilectus filius ii, *de rescriptis*, n. 2.
[79] Felinus, *o. c.*, n. 1.

position in Canon Law. In the Repertorium of the former,[80] and in the Summa of the latter [81] the domicile had achieved sufficient importance to receive exclusive explanation.

Article III.—From the Council of Trent to the New Code

It is to be remarked at the outset that, if we except its local aspect, no new notions concerning domicile were introduced during this period.[82] The theory of domicile that obtained in Roman law, and which had already been accepted by the pre-Tridentine canonists, had come to stay.

The present period, however, is not without its importance in regard to the history of domicile. In the 24th session of the Council of Trent, it was determined by the Fathers of the Council that the proper pastor of parties about to enter marriage must be present at the marriage under pain of its invalidity.[83] Although it was not decreed who the proper pastor was, immediately after the Council canonists unanimously determined that the proper pastor was the pastor of the place in which the contracting parties had a domicile.[84] This teaching received official sanction and confirmation in the Brief of Urban VIII, "Exponi Nobis" on August 14, 1627.[85] Stimu-

---

[80] Bertachinus, *Repertorium, v.* "Domicilium."

[81] *Summa Sylvestrina, v.* "Domicilium."

[82] The peculiar regulations of the Constitution "Speculatores" regarding domicile are to be understood only in regard to the reception of Orders, as the Const. itself twice declares. Cf. La Croix, *Theologia Moralis*, lib. VI, pt. II, n. 2177; Sanchez, *de Matr.*, III, 23, 7.

[83] Conc. Trid., Sess. XXIV, *de ref. matr.*, c. 1.

[84] Sanchez, *De Matrimonio* III, 23, 6 ff.

[85] Cf. *Bullarium Romanum*, Vol. XIII, p. 537.

lated by the great importance now attaching to domicile, the post-Tridentine canonists perfected and clarified the notion of domicile, brought it into harmony with ecclesiastical practice, and, with an eye to practical difficulties, evolved a fairly comprehensive system of presumptions to prove, in cases of doubt, the existence or non-existence of a domicile. The notion of domicile that obtained previous to the publication of the Code may now be presented.

§1. *General Notion and Division of Domicile*

Domicile was defined, in general, as the place of permanent habitation (*locus perpetuae habitationis*).[86] To indicate *domicile* various expressions were used, viz., *domicilium, domicilium habitationis*,[87] *habitatio*,[88] and other like expressions. As a general rule, however, the word *domicilium* was used.

While canonists generally acknowledged three distinct kinds of domicile, viz., the domicile of origin, the domicile of habitation, and the legal or necessary domicile, they did not employ a uniform manner of division. Some gave a threefold division embracing the three kinds of domicile mentioned above.[89] Others, again, divided domicile into the domicile of origin and the domicile of habitation, subdividing the latter into voluntary domicile and necessary

[86] Cf. authors passim.

[87] Sanchez, *De Matr.*, III, 23, n. 1–6; Engel, lib. II, tit. II, n. 5, 7; Reiffenstuel, lib. II, tit. II, n. 17; Pichler, *Epitome juris Canonici*, lib. II, tit, II, n. 23; Schmalzgrueber, lib. II, tit. II, n. 8.

[88] Baldus in C. 29, X, *de rescriptis*, I, 3, n. 3; Barbosa, *De off. et potest. Episcopi*, alleg. IV, n. 23.

[89] Menochius, *De. Arbitr. judic.*, lib. II, cas. 86, n. 1; Gobat, *Opera Moralia*, tr. VIII, n. 290; Passerini, *Comm. in VI°*, c. 3, *de temp. ordin.*, I, 11; D'Annibale, *Summula*, I, §83.

(legal) domicile.[90] It is to be noted that immediately following their division of domicile, the canonists emphasized the fact that when the word domicile is mentioned without a qualifying adjective, it is to be understood as the domicile of habitation.[91]

§2. *The Domicile of Origin*

The domicile of origin was defined as the place in which one was born (*locus in quo quis natus est*)[92] Before considering the notions peculiar to this kind of domicile, a few remarks may be made.

In the first place, the domicile of origin had no foundation in Roman law. It owes its existence to a misconception of the Roman *origo* by the jurist Accursius,[93] and was received into canon law by the Glossators, remaining up to the Code.[94] That the domicile of origin had no foundation in Roman law is clear from what has already been said concerning the *origo* and the domicile as they were conceived by the Roman jurists.[95]

In the second place, the *domicilium originis* is a

---

[90] Sanchez, *o. c.*, n. 4; Engel, *o. c.*, n. 5; Pirhing, lib. II, tit. II, n. 10; Reiffenstuel, *o. c.*, n. 16; Pichler, *l. c.;* Schmalzgrueber, *o. c.*, n. 8.; Maschat, *Institut. Canon.* lib. II, tit. II, n. 9; Alberti, *De domicilio ecclesiastico*, n. 1, 5.

[91] Bertachinus, *Repertorium* v. Domicilium, n. 5; Sanchez, *o. c.*, n. 7; Gutierrez, *Quaest. Canon.*, lib. III, de matr., c. 62, n. 30; Reiffenstuel, *l. c.*, Schmalzgrueber, lib. IV, tit. III, n. 145; Ojetti, *Synopsis Rerum Moralium*, n. 1880; D'Annibale, *Summula*, I, §83; nota 13.

[92] Sanchez, *o. c.*, n. 3; Barbosa, *o. c.*, n. 2; Engel, *o. c.*, n. 6; Pirhing lib. I, tit. IX, n. 21; Reiffenstuel, *o. c.*, n. 20; Maschat, lib. II, tit. II, n. 10; Alberti, *o. c.*, n. 2.

[93] Cf. above p. 36.

[94] Gloss. *oriundus* in c. 3, *de temp. ord.* in VI°, I, IX; Alberti, *l. c.* D'Annibale, *o. c.*, 1, §83.

[95] Cf. above p. 26.

misnomer. Savigny strikes the keynote when he says, "we must notice particularly a singular, but among modern writers a very common technical, expression: *domicilium originis*. According to the Roman usage, this collocation of words is contradictory as these expressions indicated two different, independent grounds of subjection."[96] Many, indeed, long before Savigny wrote, recognized this contradiction.[97] Chief among them was Chr. Thomasius, who wrote at great length, condemning those writers who placed the common domicile and domicile of origin in the same category, and gave them the same name.[98] In the light of all this, how may we explain the continued favor accorded the domicile of origin? Böckhn offers a plausible explanation. This writer, although admitting that the contention of Thomasius has the support of the written law, and that the connotation '*domicilium originis*' is less proper, yet is unwilling to expunge the term because it might beget a confusion to many readers,[99] and because, as he states, "*undique in libris occurrit.*"

Among the later canonists, Lega, D'Annibale, Ojetti, and Henry Gasparri recognize the impropriety of the expression.[100] It can hardly be doubted that what the canonists really understood by the expression *domicilium originis* was in reality the *locus originis*. Without exception they declared that the

---

[96] Savigny, *System*, VIII, §359; Cujas, *Opera Omnia*, III, col. 660.

[97] Chr. Thomasius, *de Vagabundo*, c. 1, n. 42 ff.; Voet, *Commentarius*, lib. v. tit. 1. n. 92; Huberi, *o. c.*, n. 47; Richeri, *o. c.*, v. domicilium.

[98] Thomasius, *l. c.*, Böckhn, *Comm. in jus Canon*, lib. II, tit. II, 2, n. 8 ff.

[99] Böckhn, *l. c.*

[100] Lega, *De Judiciis*, I, 339; D'Annibale, *Summula*, I, §83; Ojetti, *Synopsis*, n. 1880; H. Gasparri, *De domicilio et quasi-domicilio*, n. 44.

domicile of origin was immutable because, as they said, it was something natural, given by nature, founded in nature.[101] But this cannot be predicated of a domicile. What canonists really meant was that the locus originis cannot be changed. Thus D'Annibale very pointedly declares, "*Quod autem nostri et Canonistae impropriissime aiunt,* [*domicilium originis*] *amitti quidem posse, de ipsa origine intellegendum est.*"[102] Be all this as it may, the fact remains that the *domicilium originis* became a not entirely unimportant institution in canon law and hence must be reckoned with.

In Roman law, it has been noted, it was the legal birthplace that determined one's *origo,* i.e., not the actual place of birth, but where one should have been born—the place where the father had the "*jus civitatis.*"[103] A similar principle was adopted by most of the canonists. According to them, it was the place where the father had his domicile that determined one's *domicilium originis.*[104] Some few older canonists, however, took a different view of the matter. According to these authorities, in determining one's domicile of origin, the truth is to be considered, i.e., the actual place of birth is the decisive test, not where the child should have been born.[105] The difference of opinion seems to have arisen in determining the *origo*

---

[101] Sanchez, *o. c.*, n. 4.

[102] D'Annibale, *o. c.*, I, §83, nota 10.

[103] Cf. above p. 6.

[104] Bartolus, Comm. in D. L. 1. 6; Panormitanus in c. rodulphus, *de rescript.*, n. 9; Sanchez, *de Matr.*, III, 23, 3; Bonacina, *de Matr.*, disp. VIII, Punct. 4, n. 13; Engel, lib. I, tit. XI, n. 26; Pirhing, lib. I, tit. XI, n. 21; Laymann, *Theologia Moralis*, lib. V, tr. IX, cap. 9, n. 10.

[105] Joannes Imola and Paulus de Castro quoted by Oliva, *De foro Ecclesiae*, part III, q. 21, n. 5; Mascardus, *De probationibus*, concl. 1141.

of a child born in a certain place, outside the parental domicile, where his parents were staying for a short time, e.g., for a short vacation.

The proponents of the first opinion declared that the child's domicile of origin was the place in which, at the time of birth, the father has his domicile; not the place of actual birth. This opinion was defended by many eminent authorities, and according to Oliva, who wrote early in the eighteenth century, it was the truer, common and more received opinion.[106] According to the second opinion, the actual place of birth determined the domicile of origin. This opinion marshalled its defenders from among the ranks of the ancient canonists.[107] A third opinion, desirous of effecting a harmony between the first two, made a distinction. The child who was born "*in itinere*," as the canonists put it, was born either while the parents had a domicile, to which they will shortly return, or on the contrary he was born while his parents, having abandoned their former domicile, are migrating to another place there to constitute a domicile. In the former case, the domicile of origin of the child was the place where his parents had their domicile; in the latter case, the domicile of origin was in the place where he was actually born. This opinion Schmalzgrueber regarded as the preferable one, and it is the one that obtained previous to the Code.[108] In regard to the foregoing discussion, it would seem

---

[106] Oliva, *l. c.*; cf. authors cited in note 104.

[107] Cf. authors cited in note 105.

[108] Schmalzgrueber, lib. II, tit. II, n. 21; Maschat, lib. II, tit. II, n. 10; Alberti, *De domicilio ecclesiastico*, n. 2; D'Angelo, *Il domicilio ecclesiastico*, p. 21. Barbosa, *De off. et. potest. Epis.*, alleg. IV, n. 16; Schmier, op. cit., lib. II, tr. 1, c. 3, n. 17; P. Wiestner, *Institutiones Canonicae*, lib. II, tit. II, n. 17.

that canonists made much ado about nothing, since in connection with the proper bishop for Ordination where *origo* had its sole importance a different set of rules applied. These regulations, contained in the Constitution "*Speculatores*"[109] of Innocent XII which remained in force up to the Code, are admirably summed up by Honorante [110] in the following manner. "The general rule for determining one's *origo* as far as concerns the reception of Orders is this: At the time of the son's birth, the father did or did not have a domicile in some place. If the father had a domicile the origo of the son is the place where the father had his domicile, whether the son was born there or not. If the father did not have a domicile at the time of the son's birth, then the origo of the son is the place where the father was naturally born. In this latter case, if the father afterwards acquired a domicile in the place where the child was born, then this place, not the place where the father was born, determined the son's origo."

The following particular cases may be noted:

1. As in Roman law, the illegitimate child follows the domicile of origin of its mother.[111]

2. The foundling (*expositus*) acquires a domicile of origin in the place in which he is found.[112]

---

[109] Innocent XII, Const. "*Speculatores*," 4 Nov. 1694,—*Fontes*, n. 258.

[110] Honorante, *Praxis Secretariae Tribunalis*, cap. 1, nota 9.

[111] D. L. 1. 9. Barbosa, *o. c.*, n. 17; Pirhing, lib. I, tit. XI, n. 21; Engel, lib. I, tit. XI, n. 26; Reiffenstuel, lib. I, tit. XI, n. 92; Schmalzgrueber, lib. II, tit. II, n. 22; Alberti, *l. c.;* S. C. C. 15 Feb. 1704—Soglia, *Inst. juris Privati*, n. 44; Ojetti, *Synopsis*, n. 2973.

[112] S. C. C. 15 Feb. 1704—Soglia, *l.c.*, S.C.C. *in Urbaniten.* 4 Dec. 1762—*Thesaurus Resol. S. C. C.* XXXI, 250 ff.; Honorante, *Praxis Secretariae Tribunalis*, c. I, dub. 3; Barbosa, *l. c.;* Amostazo, *De Causis Piis*, lib. IV, c. 11, n. 76; Reiffenstuel, *l. c.*, n. 92; Ferraris, *Bibliotheca*, v. ordo, n. 21; Alberti, *l. c.;* Pirhing, lib. V. tit. XI, n. 2; Ojetti, *o. c.* n. 2975.

3. *Derelicti*, those whose parents died while they were very young, and who do not know their parents' names nor their native city, are regarded as *originarii* of that place in which they first choose a domicile.[113]

4. Neophytes acquire a domicile in the place of baptism (of spiritual generation).[114]

In Roman law, the origo was all powerful in subjecting an individual to the local jurisdiction.[115] In Canon law, its deformed offspring, the domicile of origin, had no effect except in connection with the proper bishop for the reception of Orders.[116] The unimportance of the domicile of origin in Canon law is clear from Decretal law,[117] from the unanimous consent of Canonists,[118] and from universal ecclesiastical practice.[119] As one writer puts it: "In Canon law, the '*forum originis*' without a domicile of habitation had no effect except in regard to conferring ecclesiastical Orders. According to universal practice and custom, the pastor of origin is never considered

---

113 Honorante, *l. c.*, Giraldi, *Expositio Juris Pontificii*, II, sec. 96; Gasparri, *De Sacra Ordinatione*, n. 827; Ballerini, *Opus Theologium Morale*, lib. V, tract. X, sec. VII, n. 40.

114 Paulus III Const. *Cupientes*, 21 March, 1524—*Bullarium Romanum*, VI, 336; Clement XI Const. "*Propagandae*," March, 1704,—*Bullarium Romanum*, XXI, 108; S.C.C. 15 Feb. 1704—Soglia, *l.c.*; Ojetti, *Synopsis Rerum Moralium*, n. 2975.

115 Cf. above p. 9.

116 Oliva, *de foro ecclesiae*, part III, quaest. XXI, n. 15; Schmier, *Jurisprudentia Canonico-Civilis*, lib. II, tr. 1, c. 3, n. 40 ff.; Benedict XIV, *Casus Conscientiae*, V, p. 245; Pichler, *Epitome Juris Canonici*, lib. II, tit. II, n. 23.

117 C. 5, X, *de paroch.*, III, 29; c. 20, X, *de foro comp.*, II, 2.

118 Schmalzgrueber, lib. II, tit. II, n. 23; Schmier, *l. c.;* De Angelis *Praelectiones juris canonici*, lib. II, tit. II, 1, n. 2; D'Angelo, *Il domicilio ecclesiastico*, p. 22.

119 Oliva, *o. c.*, n. 15-23; cf. also Schmalzgrueber, *l. c.*

unless he is at the same time the pastor of habitation; and custom is the best interpreter of law."[120]

§3. *Domicile of Habitation*

A. General Remarks. The domicile of habitation was generally defined as the place in which one resides with the intention of remaining there forever, if nothing unforeseen occurs (*locus in quo quis habitet, animo perpetuo manendi, nisi quid avocet*).[121] As in Roman law, the constituent elements of domicile were actual residence (*factum*) and the intention of staying forever (*animus*). Canonists were entirely and unanimously agreed in their assertion as to the absolute necessity of both.[122] The declaration of Sanchez was echoed and reechoed by every canonist of the period: "*Domicilium non solum animo, sed animo et facto constituitur.*"[123]

1. *Residence* (*commoratio-habitatio*). This element required personal physical presence in the place of domicile *per modum habitationis.* It made no difference whether one lived in his own home or in

---

[120] Oliva, *o. c.*, n. 23.

[121] Sanchez, *De Matr.*, III, 23, 1; Navarrus, *Consilia*, lib. I, *de temp. ordin.* Cons. 2; Engel, lib. I, tit. XI, n. 27; Schmalzgrueber, lib. II, tit. II, n. 8; Lega, I, 337; Wernz, *Jus Decretalium*, IV, n. 177; Alberti, *De domicilio ecclesiastico*, n. 5.

[122] Sanchez, *o. c.*, n. 2; Navarrus, *o. c.*, cons. 3; Engel, *l. c.;* Pirhing, lib. II, tit. II, n. 12; Laymann, *Theologia Moralis*, lib. V, tract, VI, c. X, n. 6; Reiffenstuel, lib. II, tit. II, n. 17; Schmalzgrueber, *o. c.*, n. 9; Zallinger, *Institutiones Juris Eccl.*, lib. I, tit. II, 1, 48; D'Annibale, *Summula*, 1, §83; Deshayes, *Questions pratique sur le mariage*, qu. I.

[123] Lega, *De Judiciis*, I, n. 337; Alberti, *l. c.;* S. R. Rota, *in Causa Gratianopolitana*, 8 April, 1913.—*S. R. Rotae decisiones*, vol. V, dec. XX, n. 7; De Angelis, *o. c.*, lib. II, tit. II, 1, n. 3; Ojetti, n. 1878; S. R. Rota *in Causa Ravennaten*, 29 Dec. 1911,—A. A. S., IV (1912), 328.

another's,[124] whether he had the greater part of his possessions here or elsewhere.[125] No other condition was required save that one really and truly constitute his habitation in a certain place.

2. *Intention*. This element was received without any change from the Roman law. Thus besides actually residing in a place, one must also have the intention of remaining there forever, unless something unforeseen calls him away.[126] Calonists interpreted the phrase "*si nihil inde avocet*" as indicating in general that it was not necessary that one have the intention of remaining under all possible circumstances.[127] As Pichler happily expresses it, "*non est necesse, ut aliquis velit absolute pro omni eventu persistere in loco, sed solum tamdiu . . : rationabilis causa inde non avocaverit, adeoque sufficit proposita perpetuitas.*"[128] Lacroix tells us that it is commonly held by Sanchez and others, that one was not prevented from having the necessary intention by the fact that he was of such a mind that he would migrate if a promotion, an office or family necessity should

---

[124] Pirhing, *l. c.;* Schmalzgrueber, *l. c.;* Pignatelli, *Consultationes Canonicae*, t. V, Cons. 79, n. 1; Alberti, *l. c.*

[125] Oliva, *De foro ecclesiae*, q. XVII, n. 1; Schmalzgrueber, *o. c.*, n. 10; Alberti, *l. c.*, Feije, *De impedimentis et dispensationibus matrimonalibus*, n. 205; Bouix, *Tract. de judic, eccl.*, pars I, sect. V, cap. IV, art. II, 1; S. R. Rota *in Causa Gratianopolitana*, 8 April, 1913—*S. R. Rotae Decisiones*, V, dec. XX, n. 7.

[126] Sanchez, *l.* c., Castropalao, *Opus Morale*, tract 26, punct. 15, n. 2; Pirhing, *l. c.;* Schmalzgrueber, *l. c.*, D'Annibale, *Summula*, I, §83; Lega, *De Judiciis*, I, n. 337; Alberti, *l. c.*

[127] Sanchez, *in Decalog.*, lib. IV, c. 39, n. 20; Castropalao, *l. c.;* La Croix, *Theologia Moralis*, lib. VI, p. III, n. 720; Pichler, *Epitome Juris Canonici*, lib. II, tit. II, n. 24; Engel, lib. I, tit. XI, n. 27; Schmalzgrueber, *l. c.;* Bouix, *l. c.*, Lega, *l. c.*

[128] Pichler, *l. c.*

call him elsewhere. If, however, one prudently foresaw that he would depart for such a reason, then his intention would remain suspended.[129] The intention of permanent residence was regarded by the canonists as so essential to the notion of domicile, that one frequently meets in their writings the expression: If one lives in a place with the intention of leaving he does not acquire a domicile, even though he remains in the place for a thousand years.[130]

B. Constitution of Domicile: As in Roman law, so also in Canon law, no lapse of time was required for the constitution of a domicile. At the very moment a person began to dwell in a place with the intention of remaining there always, he acquired a domicile. It is enough to hear Sanchez: "There is no need to dwell in a place for ten years in order to acquire a domicile, but as soon as one begins to live here with the intention of remaining, he acquires a domicile."[131] This dictum of Sanchez was the certain and unanimous teaching of canonists.[132]

C. Loss of Domicile: Canonists determined this question according to the well-known principle of law: "*omnis res per quascumque causas nascitur, per*

---

[129] La Croix, *Theologia Moralis*, lib. VI, p. II, n. 2184.

[130] Bertachinus, *Reportorium*, *v.* domicilium; Felinus in c. dilectus filius ii, *de rescript.*, n. 12; Mascardus, *De Probationibus*, concl. 535, n. 13; Menochius, *de Arbitriis Judicum*, lib. II, cas. 86, n. 17, 22; Barbosa, *De off. et pot. Epis.*, alleg. IV, n. 25; Reiffenstuel, lib. I, tit. XI, n. 96. Bartolus, the great Romanist, seems to have been the first to have used this expression (in lib. II, C. de Incolis, X, 40 (39).

[131] Sanchez, *de Matr.*, III, 23. 2.

[132] Mascardus, *De Probationibus*, concl. 535, n. 3; Engel, lib. II, tit. II, n. 7; Pirhing, lib. II, tit. II, n. 12; Schmalzgrueber, lib. II, tit. II, n. 11; D'Annibale, *Summula*, I, §83; S. R. Rota *in Causa Ravennaten*, 15 May 1911,—*A.A.S.*, III, (1911) 486.

easdem dissolvitur."[133] Therefore to lose a domicile two things were required, viz., *factum et animus*, i.e., the fact of departure and the intention of not returning. Both elements were simultaneously required.[134]

D. Plurality of Domiciles: That an individual might have more than one domicile at the same time was one of the earliest notions concerning domicile taken for granted in canon law. This principle appears for the first time in the famous chapter *Is qui* of the Liber Sextus of Boniface VIII, wherein it is stated that one could have two domiciles provided he established himself equally in two places.[135] Curiously enough, it is perhaps the most frequently mentioned notion concerning domicile to be found in the glosses.[136] Later canonists accepted this principle without question, contenting themselves with stressing the fact that a strict mathematical equality of establishment or length of residence in the different places was not necessary; moral equality sufficed.[137]

[133] Regula I in Reg. juris Greg. IX.

[134] Sanchez, *de Matr.* III, 23, 2; D'Annibale, *Summula*, I, §83, "Ideo non sufficit dicessisse, si animum revertendi habeas; nec animum discedendi in perpetuum, quoad revera discesseris." Ojetti, *Synopsis*, n. 1878; Alberti, *o. c.*, n. 5; S. R. Rota *in Causa Ravennaten*, 15 May 1911—*A.A.S.*, III, (1911), 487; S. R. Rota, *Causa Parisien*, 4 March 1916—*A.A.S.*, VIII, (1916), 367 ff.

[135] C. 2, *de sepult.*, III, 13 in VI°.

[136] Glossa in c. primatus, D. 71, v. a collega sua; Glossa in 6, C. XIII, q. 2, v. liber factus; Glossa in C. 29, X, *de rescript.*, I, 3, v. domicilium; Glossa in c. 20, X, *de foro comp.*, II, 2, v. aut domicilii; Glossa in c. 2, X, *de paroch.* III, 29, v. si alterius; Glossa in c. 3, *de temp. ordin.* I, 9, in VI°, v. domicilium; Glossa in c. execrabilis in Extrav. Joann. XXII, v. vagandi materia.

[137] Baldus, *Lectura super decretal.*, lib. I, tit. III, c. 29, n. 3; Sanchez, *De Matr.*, III, 24, 3; Menochius, *de Arbitr, Judic.*, lib. II, cas. 86, n. 2; Pirhing, lib. II, tit. II, n. 13; Schmalzgrueber, lib. II, tit. II, n. 13;

E. Lack of Domicile: The fact that one could be without a domicile was acknowledged by all canonists.[138] Little comment was made. The principle was stated, and the example of the traveler of Ulpian was given as an illustration.[139] One canonist, however, Begnudelli,[140] strikes a note generally disregarded by the others. According to this writer, the fact of being without a domicile (*vagitas, vagatio*) is something that is not to be presumed; on the contrary, it must be fully proved.[141] In more recent years, just before the Code, this teaching has been emphasized in no uncertain terms by the Officials of the Sacred Roman Rota, and has been embodied by them as a principle in some recent decisions involving the validity of marriages.[142] The burden of their teaching is summed up in a decision given on March 4, 1916 in a Paris case: "*Vagitas enim in jure est res valde odiosa . . . cum status vagi sit extraordinarius et minime praesumendus.*"[143]

Wiestner, *Institutiones Canonicae*, lib. II, tit. II, n. 28; D'Annibale, *Summula*, I, §83, nota 23; S. R. Rota *in Causa Gratianapolitana*, 8 April 1913,—*Decisiones S. R. Rotae*, vol. V, dec. XX, n. 5; S. R. Rota *in Causa Ravennaten*, 15 May, 1911,—*A.A.S.*, III, (1911), p. 486.

[138] Cf. Sanchez, *de Matr.* III, 25, n. 1-3; Pirhing, lib. II, tit. II, n. 13; Schmalzgrueber, lib. II, tit. II, n. 18; Benedict XIV, *Inst. Eccl.*, Inst. XXXIII, n. 10; D'Annibale, *Summula*, I, §83.

[139] D. L. 1. 27. 2.

[140] Begnudelli-Bassi, *Bibliotheca juris canonico-civilis practica*, v. "Vagus."

[141] Begnudelli-Bassi, *l. c.*

[142] S. R. Rota, *in Causa Parisien*, 27 Jan. 1912—*A.A.S.*, IV, (1912), 277 ff.; S. R. Rota, *in Causa Parisien.*, 4 March 1916—*A.A.S.*, VIII, (1916), 367 ff.

[143] S. R. R. *in Causa Parisien*, 4 March 1916—*A.A.S.*, VIII, (1916), p. 367.

§4. *Legal or Necessary Domicile*

The legal or necessary domicile was defined as that which one necessarily obtains by disposition of law, either by reason of a bond with another person (*mulier nupta*), by reason of an office *per se* permanent (*clericus beneficiatus*), or by reason of one's condition or state of life (*relegatus, filiusfamilias*).[144] It made no difference whether the person actually lived in the place of necessary domicile or not. It mattered not even if he had a contrary intention. In the different cases, the law itself supplied either the habitation or the intention, or both.[145] The necessary domicile ceased immediately upon the cessation of the fact which is required as a condition that the law, or the will of the legislator be observed. That it really be lost, however, one must really abandon it, give it up; otherwise this necessary domicile will be thought to have passed into a voluntary domicile, and its retention will be presumed, so long as it is not certain that it has been given up.[146]

The following persons were commonly regarded as possessing necessary domiciles:

A. The Married Woman. The married woman obtained the domicile of her husband.[147] This domicile

---

[144] Passerini, *o. c.*, in c. cum nullus, n. 29; Schmalzgrueber, lib. II, tit. II, n. 14; Bouix, *l. c.*, 1; Lega, *De Judiciis*, I, 340; Wernz, *Jus Decretalium*, IV, n. 177, nota 190; Alberti, *De domicilio ecclesiastico*, n. 5; S. R. Rota *in Causa Ravennaten*, 15 May, 1911—*A.A.S.* III, (1911) 487.

[145] Wernz, *l. c.;* Alberti, *l. c.*

[146] Alberti, *l. c.*, S. R. Rota *in Causa Ravennaten*, 15 May 1911,—*A.A.S.* III, (1911), 487.

[147] C. 3, de sepult., III, 12, in VI°; Panormitanus in c. conquestus, *de foro comp.*, n. 7; Schmalzgrueber, lib. IV, tit. I, n. 350, "Effectus

she retained even in the event of her husband's death, provided she did not enter into a new marriage.[148] The principle, however, that the wife retained the domicile of her husband became ineffective in two cases, viz., in the event of lawful separation *a mensa et thoro*, and in the event of malicious desertion on the part of the husband.[149]

B. Children (*Filiifamilias*): In Roman law, the child (*filiusfamilias*), at least if he had attained the age of puberty, could acquire a domicile of his own, a domicilium proprium, voluntarium.[150] This principle was admitted in Canon law by many canonists and theologians until the time of St. Alphonsus. The words of Gobat[151] sum up the teaching of these writers on this point: "Children who have not yet attained the age of puberty are considered to have the same domicile as their father, since they cannot choose one for themselves. After the age of puberty, however, these children can make that free choice, even though they are still minors (*filiifamilias*)."[152] This teaching received confirmation in two decisions

---

proprius (matrimonii) ex parte uxoris est, quod acquirat domicilium mariti et retinet hoc mariti sui domicilium etiam marito mortuo, quamdiu manet vidua."; D'Annibale, *Summula*, I, §83, nota 16.

[148] Schmalzgrueber, *l. c.*, Feije, *De Imped. et disp. matr.*, n. 204; Lega, *De Judiciis*, I, n. 340.

[149] Feije, *l. c.;* Lega, *l. c.;* Gasparri, *de Matr.*, n. 1168; Wernz, *Jus Decretalium*, V. n. 286; Instr. S. C. de Prop. Fide, 1883, art. 2—*Coll. S. C. de Prop. Fide.* n. 1573.

[150] D. L. 1. 3; Cf. page 20.

[151] Gobat, *Opera Moralia*, VIII, n. 299.

[152] Navarrus, *Consilia*, lib. I, de temp. ordin., cons. 3, n. 6 ff.; Gobat, *l. c.;* Castropalao, *Opus Morale*, de sacr. ord., tract. XXVII, disp. 1, punct. 4; Laymann, *Theologia Moralis*, lib. V, tr. 9, cap. 9, n. 11; Passerini, *Comm. in Sexto*, c. 3, de temp. ordin., n. 52; Pirhing, lib. I, tit. XI, n. 32; St. Alphonsus, *Theologia Moralis*, lib. VI, tr. V, n. 778.

of the Sacred Congregation of the Council.[153] In one of these decrees, after this teaching is stated, a list of authorities defending it is drawn up, and there is nothing in the decree which would indicate that it was not the accepted teaching.[154] In the light of all this, one is surprised to discover, in the space of a few years and with no apparent reason, an entirely different principle coming to the fore and remaining in pacific possession up to the Code. This principle is that until children attained their majority they acquired and necessarily retained the domicile of their parents. This principle was held by a great many prominent canonists,[155] and was adopted by the officials of the Roman Rota in some recent cases regarding the validity of marriages.[156]

C. Religious were regarded by some canonists as possessing a necessary domicile in the monastery to which they were attached. They retained this domicile until they were transferred to another monastery by their superior.[157]

---

153 S.C.C. *in Bononien,* 14 Nov. 1733,—*Thesaurus Resol. S.C.C.* t. VI, p. 163. "Caeterum posse Filiusfamilias post pubertatem domicilium sibi constituere et domicilii jura nancisci ubicumque voluerit, etiam seorsim a patre, aperte habetur in ll. Placet et Non utique ff. ad municip." S.C.C. *in Ravennaten,* 28 Sept. 1743,—*Thesaurus Resol. S.C.C.*, t. XI, p. 131 ff.

154 S.C.C. *In Ravennaten,* 28 Sept. 1743, *l. c.*

155 D'Annibale, *Summula,* I, §83, nota 17; Feije, *De imped. et dispens. matr.*, n. 204; Gasparri, *De Matrimonio,* n. 925; Wernz, *Jus Decretalium,* IV, n. 177; Alberti, *De domicilio ecclesiastico,* n. 5; D'Angelo, *Il domicilio ecclesiastico,* p. 37.

156 S. R. Rota *in Causa Ravennaten,* 15 May 1911,—*A.A.S.*, III, (1911), 483; S. R. Rota *in Causa Parisien,* 27 Jan. 1912—*A.A.S.*, IV, (1912), 281; S. R. Rota *in Causa Parisien,* 4 March 1916—*A.A.S.*, VIII, (1916), 367.

157 Alberti, *De domicilio ecclesiastico,* n. 5; D'Angelo, *Il domicilio ecclesiastico,* p. 37.

D. Clerics, according to some writers, obtained a necessary domicile in the place where they had a benefice, provided the benefice was one requiring residence.[158]

§5. *The Special Domicile for Ordination*

Until the publication of the Constitution "*Speculatores*" of Innocent XII on the 4th of November, 1694,[159] the ordinary domicile of habitation sufficed to subject an individual to a bishop for the reception of orders.[160]

The Constitution "*Speculatores*," however, introduced a new order of things. The ordinary domicile was no longer sufficient. There was required an altogether special domicile—a *domicilium qualificatum*. The elements constitutive of every domicile, viz., residence and intention, were of course required. But, to be lawfully invoked in view of ordination, the domicile had to be endowed with certain special characteristics or qualities. An examination of the "*Speculatores*" reveals two ways of acquiring this *domicilium qualificatum* necessary for the licit reception of orders. The first way of acquiring this special domicile was by a residence of ten years in a place, accompanied by an oath to remain there permanently.[161] The second way of acquiring this domicile was by the transference of the greater part

---

[158] Alberti, *l. c.;* D'Angelo, *l. c.*

[159] Innocent XII, Const. "*Speculatores*,"—*Fontes*. n. 258.

[160] Reiffenstuel, lib. I, tit. XI, n. 88 ff.; Riganti, *in Regulae Canc. Apost.*, Reg. 24, III, n. 45.

[161] Innocent XII, Const. "*Speculatores*," art. 5; Honorante, *Praxis Secretariae Tribunalis*, cap. 9, nota 4; Gasparri, *De Ordinatione*, n. 830; Many, *Praelectiones de Ordinatione*, n. 33; Wernz, *Jus Decretalium*, II, n. 28.

of one's possessions to a place, together with residence for a considerable length of time,[162] accompanied, as above, by an oath to remain permanently.[163] This *domicilium qualificatum* for orders remained in force until the publication of the Code.[164] It is important to note that the regulations of the Constitution "*Speculatores*" had no influence on the general notion of domicile; nor did they have any effect except in regard to the reception of orders, as the Constitution itself twice declares.[165]

§6. *Place of Domicile*

While canonists generally were in agreement regarding most questions connected with the notion of domicile, a sharp controversy existed, especially in more recent times, concerning the place of domicile (*locus domicilii*).

In Roman law, according to what was considered the better opinion, the place of domicile was the city (*civitas, municipium*), not the province.[166] The earliest positive ecclesiastical legislation on the matter is in perfect accord with the accepted theory in Roman law. In the famous chapter *Is qui*,[167] of Boniface

---

[162] This considerable length of time was commonly regarded as three years. Cf. Honorante, *l. c.;* Riganti, *o. c.*, n. 46; Gasparri, *o. c.*, n. 832; Many, *l. c.;* Wernz, *l. c.*

[163] Innocent XII, const. "*Speculatores*," art. 5; Honorante, *l. c.;* Gasparri, *o. c.*, 830–832; Many, *l. c.;* Wernz, *l. c.*

[164] Wernz, *Jus Decretalium*, II, n. 28; D'Angelo, *Il domicilio ecclesiastico*, p. 103 ff.

[165] Cf. La Croix, *Theologia Moralis*, lib. VI, part II, n. 2177; Many, *l. c.*

[166] Cf. above p. 24.

[167] C. 3, *de sepulturis*, III, 12, in VI°.

VIII, the city domicile is expressly acknowledged,[168] but no official mention is made of any other.

Together with the domicile in the city, frequent mention is also made of a domicile in a diocese or in a parish, especially in the *Glossae* on the *Corpus Juris Canonici* and in the writings of the pre-Tridentine canonists.[169] In this connection it is to be noted that the Glossators and the Commentators regarded the the words *paroecia* and *diocesis* as interchangeable terms. Thus, for example, Hostiensis uses the expression "parishioners of a diocese," and expressly declares that an episcopate is also called a parish.[170] Until the Council of Trent, then, it would seem that, although the domicile in the city had the support of positive legislation, the domicile in the diocese and in the parish did not lack defenders.

After the Council of Trent, as a result of the new matrimonial legislation[171] there was a definite trend towards a parochial domicile, and from that time until the new Code the majority of Canonist concluded that a domicile could be acquired only in a parish.[172] The domicile in the diocese and in the

---

[168] C. 3, *de sepulturis*, III, 12 in VI°, "Is qui habet domicilium in civitate."

[169] Gloss on c. statutum, *de rescript.*, I, 3, in VI°, *v.* ejusdem civitatis; Gloss on c. 1, *de foro competente*, II, 2 in VI° *v.* contrahentes; Hostiensis, Comm. in c. 2, X, *de parochiis*, III, 29; Felinus, in c. dilectus filius ii, *de rescript.*, n. 13.

[170] Hostiensis, in c. 20, X, *de decimis*, III, 30; c. 4, X, *de parochiis*, III, 29. "Episcopatus parochia appellatur." Cf. Glossa in C. 2, 3 *de temp. ordin.*, I, 11, in VI°.

[171] Conc. Trid., Sess. XXIV, *De reform. Matr.* c. 1.

[172] Cf. Gasparri, *De Matr.*, n. 916; D'Annibale, *Summula*, I, §83, nota 8; Farren, *Domicile and Quasi-domicile*, p. 37; Wernz, Votum—*Anal. Eccl.*, vol. 7, p. 66, n. 14, 15; Boudinhon, *Quelques reflexions sur le domicile*,—*Canoniste Contemporain*, vol. XXII (1899) p. 204 ff.

city, however, did not lack defenders. Deschamps,[173] and Lombardi[174] vigorously defended a diocesan domicile even for matrimonial purposes, while many other prominent authorities including Gennari,[175] D'Angelo [176] and Langonio,[177] admitted a diocesan domicile, at least for the reception of orders.

The domicile in the city also enlisted the authority of not a few eminent canonists, including Sanchez [178] and Benedict XIV[179] among the older canonists, and Laurentius[180] and Lehmkuhl[181] among the more recent writers.

More recent developments, in the form of particular replies of the Holy See and the stylus of the Roman Rota, tend to rule out the domicile in the diocese or in the city, or at least do not recognize them as part of domiciliary discipline.

A Reply of the Congregation of the Council to the Bishops of the United States clearly implies that the Congregation was not in favor of the diocesan domicile. The Bishops had requested the Holy See to decree that those who passed from one *diocese* to another, certain conditions being fulfilled, be regarded as having a domicile in the latter *diocese*. The Congregation replied that in the circumstances stated "those passing from one *place* . . . to another,

---

[173] Cf. *Can. Contemp.*, vol. XXIII (1900) p. 385, ff., esp. p. 401.

[174] *Inst. Juris Canonici Privati*, III, p. 188.

[175] *Quistioni Canoniche*, q. 211.

[176] *Il domicilio ecclesiastico*, p. 109.

[177] Votum—*Anal. Eccl.*, vol. XIII, p. 385.

[178] *De Matrimonio*, III, 23, 14.

[179] *Inst. Eccl.*, Inst. XXXIII, n. 8.

[180] *Inst. Juris Eccl.* n. 584.

[181] *Theol. Moral.* II, n. 889.

may be considered to have acquired a domicile there for purposes of marriage."[182]

In 1898, the Archbishop of Paris requested the same Congregation to recognize a diocesan domicile in favor of those who, although residing for a number of years in the diocese of Paris, yet had not remained in any parish long enough to acquire there a domicile or quasi-domicile. The Congregation, however, refused to recognize any domicile or quasi-domicile save a parochial one.[183]

The officials of the Rota, in a number of recent matrimonial cases, have also looked with disfavor on the diocesan and city domicile. Thus in a Ravenna case[184] decided on May 15, 1911, the Auditors of the Rota declared that according to Canon law the domicile or quasi-domicile is established by residence in a parish, not in a diocese; just as in civil law it is established by residence in a commonwealth or city, not in a province.

This principle was again declared on at least two other occasions.[185]

Despite the evident mind of the Roman authorities, the diocesan and city domicile were not entirely abandoned, and thus matters stood up to the Code.[186]

---

[182] *Collectanea S.C.P.F.* n. 1413.

[183] Cf. *Anal. Eccl.*, vol. VII (1899), p. 6; cf. Lega, *De Judiciis*, I, n. 338, nota 1: "Hodie contraria opinio dicenda sit omino reprobanda, quippe eam repudiavit S.C.S. off. . . . Nov. 9, 1898."

[184] S.R.R., *in Causa Ravennaten*, 15 May, 1911,—A.A.S., III, (1911), 486.

[185] S.R.R. *Causa Ravennaten*, 29 Dec. 1911,—*A.A.S.*, vol. VI, (1914), p. 327; S.R.R. *Causa Parisien*, *4 March 1916*—*A.A.S.*, vol. VIII, (1916), p. 369.

[186] Cf. De Smet, *De Sponsalibus et Matrimonio*, (ed. 1912), n. 73.

§7. *The Effects of Domicile*

The principal effect of domicile in Canon law, as in Roman law, consisted in the subjection of the individual to the local laws and jurisdiction of the place of his domicile.[187] In particular, by domicile an individual secured his proper bishop,[188] and his proper pastor [189] for the exercise of his diocesan and parochial rights and duties.

---

[187] Panormitanus in c. fin. *de paroch.*, n. 4; Navarrus, *Consilia*, lib. IV, de const. n. 5; Bertachinus, *Reportorium*, v. Domicilium; D'Angelo, *Il domicilio ecclesiastico*, p. 40; Alberti, *De domicilio ecclesiastico*, n. 9.

[188] C. 3, *de temp. ordin.*, I, 11 in VI°; c. 20, X, *de foro comp.*, II, 2; Felinus, in dilectus filius ii, *de Rescript.*; n. 10; Schmalzgrueber, lib. II, tit. II, n. 23; Wernz, *Jus Decretalium*, V, n. 284.

[189] Glossa in c. 2, *de sepult.*, III, 12 in VI°; Sanchez, *de Matr.* III, 23, 7; Navarrus, *de poenit*, dist. VI, c. Placuit, n. 102; Oliva, *de foro ecclesiae*, p. III, q. 21, n. 17, "Quoad jura parochialia jus canonicum domicilium habitationis tantum consideravit . . . et sic universalis praxis observat." D'Annibale, *Summula*, I, §§85, 86.

CHAPTER III

QUASI-DOMICILE BEFORE THE CODE

Canon law, as we have seen, had no independent and original theory of domicile, but borrowed, in substance at least, the theory of domicile that obtained in Roman law.[1]

Canon law, however, developed the idea of domicile to a greater extent, in the sense that it gave to persons, even tho not permanently established in a place, what came to be known as quasi-domicile. The quasi-domicile, then, is of strictly ecclesiastical origin. Both the name, quasi-domicile, and the *concept of quasi-domicile*, i.e., residence with the intention of remaining for the greater part of a year, were unknown to the Roman jurists.

The quasi-domicile in canon law, as the domicile in Roman law, was evolved to meet practical needs and difficulties. Unlike the domicile, however, the quasi-domicile was not the result of direct legislation but was developed almost entirely by the canonists. For this reason the idea grew very slowly, and for a long time the theory of quasi-domicile remained vague and undetermined.

Article I.—From the Beginning to the Council of Trent

Curiously enough the expression, quasi-domicile, and the concept, or at least the germ of the concept,

[1] Cf. Wernz, Votum—*Anal. Eccl.*, Vol. VII, p. 66, n. 13.

have come down to us thru two entirely different channels. The former developed in connection with the proper forum in ecclesiastical trials. The latter had its origin in the attempt to determine a proper pastor for certain classes of people, e.g., merchants, in regard to the discharge of their parochial rights and obligations.

§1. *The Expression—Quasi-Domicile*

The Roman law had no knowledge of the quasi-domicile. Nevertheless it provided the occasion, which caused a discussion, out of which the expression quasi-domicile sprang into being.

In a law of the Justinian Code, which discusses the forum of senators and other public officials, it was decreed that these persons should respond in the place "*ubi majorem bonorum partem possident et assidue conversantur.*"[2] Innocent IV commenting on the title "*De foro competente*" of the Decretals of Gregory IX, and discussing in particular the forum of domicile, sets out to explain this Roman law. According to Innocent a domicile could be constituted either by the transference of the greater part of one's possessions to a place or by continuous residence (*assidua conversatio*).[3] This latter circumstance is particularly stressed. In support of his contention, Innocent alleges the *glossa* on another law of the Justinian Code, which deals with the crime of kidnapping. This law states that the competent judge in a case of this kind is the judge of the place where the criminal happens to be staying, "*ubi degit.*" According to the glossator the words "*ubi degit*"[4]

[2] C. III, 24. 2.

[3] Comm. in c. ex parte B., de *foro competente.*

[4] C. III, 15. 2.

signify the place where one has his domicile or where one is sojourning even though he has not a domicile in the place.[5]

Hostiensis [6] accepted the teaching of Innocent, but Bartolus, the civilian, while willing to concede that a person acquired a forum by reason of continuous residence, was unwilling to grant him a domicile.[7]

Panormitanus, the great canonist of the fifteenth century, took a middle course between the opinions of Innocent and Bartolus. By continuous residence one did not establish a true domicile; rather did he acquire a quasi-domicile.[8] Just exactly what Panormitanus meant by this expression is difficult to say. He gives no definition of the term, but in his explanation the following facts are fairly clear. The residence necessary to constitute a quasi-domicile is something less than ten years, for by reason of this residence, Panormitanus says, "*sortitur scholaris domicilium.*"[9] Again, there is no question of a mere transient delay in a place.[10] According to Panormitanus, then, in order to acquire a quasi-domicile a constant sojourn is required. A residence of ten years is not necessary; a mere passing stay will not suffice. There is not the slightest hint of the necessity of intention.

Felinus Sandaeus, who wrote towards the end of the fifteenth century, gives a summary of the conflicting opinions, and concludes "*Potest dici, quod*

---

[5] Glossa in *C.* III, 15. 2.

[6] Comm. in c. omnis, *de poenit. et remiss.* n. 23.

[7] Comm. in *C.* III. 15. 2.

[8] Comm. in c. quod clericis, de foro comp., n. 4.—"nota quod ex solo commorari in loco, quis contrahit saltem *quasi domicilium.*"

[9] *Ibidem.*

[10] *Ibidem.*

scholares et mercatores et similes illis assidue conversantes dicuntur contrahere saltem quasi domicilium."[11] Ungarellis [12] and Navarrus [13] content themselves with merely mentioning the expression and referring it to Panormitanus.

§2. *The Concept of Quasi-Domicile*

The chief effect of domicile in Canon Law was to attach a person to a certain parish and diocese, thereby subjecting him to the jurisdiction of a certain pastor and bishop.[14] In the general run of affairs there would be no difficulty about this arrangement. Most people of this period were not afflicted with the mobility of the modern citizen, and the constitution of a domicile as a means of subjection was not too much to ask. There were, however, certain classes of people, e.g., students, merchants and similar groups, who were accustomed to remain in a place for a considerable length of time, without, however, the intention of permanently residing there, and hence without acquiring a domicile. It would be difficult for them to always approach the parish church of domicile to discharge their various parochial obligations, and it was quite reasonable that they be permitted to discharge them and become quasi parishioners in places of less stable residence. The fulfillment of the precept of annual confession and Paschal communion[15] was calculated to work an especial hardship on these classes of people.

---

[11] Comm. in c. dilectus filius, *de rescript.* n. 13.

[12] Cf. additio in *Summa Angelica* v. Domicilium.

[13] Comm. in c. Placuit, dist.VI, *de Poenit.* n. 89.

[14] Panormitanus in lib. III, tit. 29, c. 5. n. 4; Sanchez, *De Matrimonio*, III, 23, 7; D'Annibale, *Summula*, I, 85, 86.

[15] Conc. Lateran. IV, c. 21—Mansi, XXII, 1007.

It is in the attempt to provide a convenient *modus agendi* for the above-mentioned classes of people that we are to find the seed whence was to spring the notion of quasi-domicile.

Curiously enough, it is in the writings of Innocent IV that we are to notice first a departure from the idea that the domicile alone gave parochial competence. Commenting on the chapter "*Omnis utriusque,*"[16] Innocent declared that yearly students and merchants should confess to the pastor of the place in which they resided for a year, and by him they can be absolved. In confirmation of this teaching, Innocent appeals to the chapter "*Questi*" of the decree of Gratian.[17]

Hostiensis[18] and, following and alleging him, Paludanus[19] merely repeat and confirm the teaching of Innocent.

Paul de Leazariis, discussing another field of parochial competence, viz., ecclesiastical burial, declares that in the case of a person who dies in a parish in which he has resided for at least a year, the canonical portion should be divided between his first parochial church and that in which he died.[20]

The testimony of Petrus de Ubaldis is most interesting. According to this writer a person becomes a parishioner when he either dwells, or intends to dwell in a place, for a year or for the greater part of a year.[21] One cannot but remark the striking re-

---

[16] C. 12, X, *De poenit. et remiss.* V, 38.

[17] C. 46, C. XVI, q. 1.

[18] In c. omnis, *de poenit. et remiss.* n. 23.

[19] *Commentaria in Sent.*, Dist. XVII n. IV.

[20] Apud Panormitanus in c. in nostra, *de sepult.* n. 10.

[21] *De Canonica Epsicop.* C. 7 n. 2. "Parochianus dicitur, quando per annum vel majoren anni partem inhabitet, aut inhabitare intendit."

semblance this statement of Ubaldis bears to the present law of the Code.

Panormitanus is the next canonist to engage our attention. Before replying directly to the question: who is the proper pastor for scholars, Panormitanus makes a distinction between the necessary sacraments, e.g., confession, and the voluntary sacraments and other voluntary actions, e.g., dispensation from vows.[22] For the discharge of the voluntary obligations, Panormitanus declared that the pastor of domicile alone was the proper pastor.[23] In regard to the necessary sacraments, present habitation was sufficient to constitute one a parishioner.[24]

Joannes de Clavasio, author of the *Summa Angelica*, and Sylvester Prieras, author of the *Summa Sylvestrina*, adopted both the distinctions and the conclusions of Panormitanus. However, where Panormitanus speaks indefinitely of present habitation (*habitatio de presenti*), these writers are much more precise. The testimony of both is practically the same. In ordinary cases, declares the Summa Angelica, one becomes a parishioner by the constitution of a domicile.[25] One becomes a parishioner in regard to the necessary sacraments when he resides in a place for the greater part of a year, i.e., for more than six months, even though he has not constituted a domicile.[26]

The view of Navarrus in this matter is important

---

[22] Panormitanus, Comm. in c. cum nullus, *de temp. ordin.*

[23] Panormitanus, *l. c.*

[24] Comm. in c. omnis, *de poenit. et remiss.* n. 23. Panormitanus cites Federicus de Senis as the sponsor of this opinion.

[25] *Summa Angelica* v. Parochia; *Summa Sylvestrina* v. Parochia.

[26] *Summa Angelica, l. c.*; *Summa Sylvestrina, l. c.*

by reason of the fact that it influenced a number of canonists of the following period. Navarrus declared that the term "*incolae*" embraced not only those who had a domicile in a place, but also those who resided there for some period of time, of such length, that in the estimation of prudent men, they could be regarded as inhabitants (*habitatores*).

Mascardus [27] and Menochius,[28] the last important writers of this period, are one in declaring that a parishioner is one who dwells in a place for the greater part of the year.

Thus far, two things are especially to be noted. In the first place, we have seen the origin of the expression—quasi-domicile. In the mind of Panormitanus, the only canonist to discuss it at length, it connoted a residence that was not sufficient to constitute a domicile, but at the same time was more than a passing stay. Secondly, in an effort to provide for the convenient discharge of parochial obligations on the part of certain classes of people, we have noticed that beginning with Innocent IV and ending with Mascardus and Menochius, canonists commonly held that persons, who resided in a place for at least the greater part of a year, were to be regarded as parishioners.

In conclusion, it may be stated that at this time the quasi-domicile and the habitation for the greater part of a year were not equivalent ideas. The fusion of the two was to be accomplished by a canonical genius of the period directly following the Council of Trent, Thomas Sanchez.

---

[27] Mascardus, *De Probationibus*, concl. 588 and 1145.

[28] Menochius, *De Praesumptionibus*, l. VI, praes. 88.

Article II.—From the Council of Trent to the New Code

§ 1. *From the Council of Trent to the Decree of 1867*

It is only natural to suppose that the new matrimonial legislation of the Council of Trent [29] would give a great impetus to the development of the idea of granting parochial rights to those residing in a place for the greater part of a year. The same difficulties and inconvenience consequent upon fulfillment of the Lateran law would be felt also in regard to the fulfillment of the decree "*Tametsi.*" Besides, in this latter case there was question of the validity of a sacrament which affected Christian life to a very great degree.

The Council of Trent, as already noticed, declared merely that for a marriage to be valid, it must be celebrated before the proper pastor of at least one of the contracting parties,[30] leaving the determination of the proper pastor to canonists. These latter quickly determined that the proper pastor was the pastor of the place in which one had a domicile,[31] and their teaching was confirmed by the Brief of Urban VIII, "*Exponi Nobis,*" 14 August, 1627.[32]

But what about the pastor of the place in which a person resided for the greater part of the year, e.g., a servant or a scholar? Canonists commonly had decided that he was the proper pastor for the administration of the sacraments of Penance and

[29] Conc. Trid., Sess. XXIV, *de reform. matr.*, c. 1.

[30] Conc. Trid. Sess. XXIV, *de reform. matr.*, c. 1.

[31] Cf. Sanchez, *De Matrimonio*, III, disp. 23, n. 7.

[32] Urban VIII, "*Exponi Nobis.*"—*Bullarium Romanum*, XIII, 537.

the Eucharist.[33] Not a few had declared that the canonical portion was to be divided between this pastor and the pastor of domicile.[34] Was this pastor competent also to assist at the marriage of such residents? Thomas Sanchez, one of the first canonists to write after the Council of Trent, discusses this question at great length in his celebrated treatise *De Matrimonio.*[35]

In an effort to determine the proper pastor for assistance at marriage, Sanchez weighs four cases: (1) those who have a domicile in a certain place; (2) those who have no domicile; (3) those who have a domicile in one place and who go to another place for a short time, e.g., *causa recreationis;* (4) those who have a domicile in one place and who go to another place intending to reside there (ibi habitaturus) for a certain length of time, to return afterwards to their domicile, e.g., scholars, servants and other similar groups of people.[36] In the first two cases the usual rules apply. In the third case, Sanchez, arguing from the chapter "*Is qui,*"[37] decides that the person is a parishioner only in the place where he has his domicile, and not that to which he goes "*causa recreationis.*"[38] The whole difficulty, Sanchez states, lies in the fourth case, and in this there are two opinions.

[33] Innocent IV, Comm. in c. 12, *de poenit et remiss.* X, V, 38; *Summa Angelica* v. Parochia; *Summa Sylvestrina* v. Domicilium; Panormitanus, Comm. in c. omnis, *de poenit. et remiss.* n. 23; Sanchez, *De Matr.* III, 23, n. 12.

[34] Panormitanus, in c. in nostra, *de sepult.*, n. 10, where Paul de Leazariis is cited as defending this teaching.

[35] Sanchez, *De Matrimonio,* lib. III, disp. XXIII.

[36] Sanchez, *l. c.*

[37] C. 3, *de sepult.*, III, 12, in VI°.

[38] Sanchez, *l. c.*

According to the first opinion, which Sanchez calls most probable, only those who have a domicile in a place can be regarded as parishioners there, and hence the pastor of the place of domicile, and he alone, can assist at the marriage. He is the proper pastor. The chapter "*Is qui*"[39] and a list of authorities are cited in support of this view.[40]

According to the second view, which Sanchez thinks is the truer one, and which he embraces, a person becomes a parishioner in a place by reason of habitation when that is not for a short time. The habitation which, for example, students have in the place of studies and which servants have in the place of their employer, is sufficient to constitute one a parishioner. The duration of the habitation required is more definitely stated in the following argument, which, it may be noted, appears to be the principal one: He is the proper pastor for assistance at marriage who, in the chapter "*Omnis utriusque,*"[41] is called the proper pastor for annual confession and paschal communion; but this latter is the pastor of that parish in which one resides for the greater part of the year. Therefore, the pastor of the parish in which a person resides for the greater part of the year is the proper pastor for assistance at marriage.[42] As proof of his minor Sanchez appeals to the authority of those canonists already mentioned in the preceding period.[43] Other arguments offered by Sanchez in support of his

---

[39] C. 3, *de sepult.*, III, 12, in VI°.

[40] Sanchez, *o. c.*, n. 11 ff.

[41] C. 12, X, *de poenit. et remiss.*, V, 38.

[42] Sanchez, *o. c.*, n. 12.

[43] Cf. page 70ff.

assertion are based on a number of chapters of the Decretals.[44]

In the present discussion the word quasi-domicile occurs several times, and although its connection with the idea of residence for the greater part of the year is undoubtedly implied,[45] it is in a preceding disputation that their equivalent meaning is expressly stated.[46] It is here also that we find a clear exposition of Sanchez' theory of quasi-domicile.

Sanchez is seeking to determine what residence is necessary that a person be obliged to observe the laws and customs of a place. He gives the various opinions and then states: "In my opinion, in order that a person be bound by the laws and customs of a place, it suffices that he intend to dwell here for the greater part of the year (*ut ibi sit habitaturus majore anni parte*). For this suffices to constitute a domicile, not a domicile '*simpliciter*', but a quasi-domicile for the necessary sacraments. . . . This also suffices to constitute a quasi-domicile for the voluntary sacraments (excepting the sacrament of Holy Orders), and to obtain a dispensation from the local bishop. Again, a more suitable and convenient arrangement cannot be conceived to avoid two extremes, viz., that the intention of permanent residence is necessary, or that a mere passing stay is sufficient. Finally, in the judgment of prudent men, one is said to intend to reside in a certain place (*habitaturus in aliquo loco*) who intends to establish himself there for the greater part of the year (*qui majore anni parte in eo sedem constituturus sit*).

[44] C. 11, X, *de sepult.*, III, 28; c. 46, C. XVI, q. 1.

[45] Sanchez, *l. c.*

[46] Sanchez, *o. c.* disp. XVIII.

This, however, must be observed, namely, that he who comes to a place with the intention of living there the greater part of the year, is bound from the very first day of his arrival to observe the laws and customs of the place, because from that moment he has placed the required conditions."[47] This statement of Sanchez is quite clear. Any attempt at interpretation would result in mere repetition.

While the position of Sanchez on the nature of the residence cannot be questioned, one writer, Fourneret,[48] is of the opinion that Sanchez does not state with sufficient clearness whether intention is required for the constitution of a quasi-domicile, or whether sole habitation of fact suffices. He mentions, in particular, that Sanchez in attempting to deduce arguments from the Decretals uses the expressions: "*ubi sola habitatio et non animus ponderatur*" and "*assiduc habitare.*" It may be remarked in the beginning that the expressions to which Fourneret calls attention are not original with Sanchez. The first expression was used by Federicus de Senis,[49] and the second was borrowed from the Roman law by Panormitanus[50] and Felinus,[51] and used by them in connection with development of quasi-domicile. They were employed by these writers to denote opposition to domicile at a time when quasi-domicile was quite a vague term, and when the idea of yearly residence, without the slightest hint of intention, was beginning

---

[47] Sanchez, *o. c.*, disp. XVIII, n. 9.

[48] Fourneret, *Le Domicile Matrimonial*, p. 115.

[49] Federicus de Senis apud Panormitanus, Comm., in c. in nostra, *de sepulturis.*

[50] Panormitanus, Comm. in c. quod clericis, *de foro comp.*, n. 4.

[51] Felinus in c. dilectus filius, *de rescriptis*, n. 11.

to rear its head. It is quite possible that Sanchez was merely referring to them, expressions long in use, without attaching too great significance to them.

But whatever of this, while not stated with a nice exactness in his treatise on Matrimony, it is quite clear that Sanchez required intention besides actual residence. In the first place, in the observation contained in the latter part of the quotation referred to above,[52] Sanchez declares that when a person comes to a place with the intention of staying the greater part of a year, he has the *conditions required* to constitute a domicile. Surely the mind of Sanchez is clear from this statement. The intention to remain is a required condition.

Again, in his *Opus Morale in Pracepta Decalogi*, there is a very clear statement from Sanchez on the point.[53] Discussing the subjection necessary that a person may obtain a dispensation from a bishop, Sanchez declares that some authorities require a domicile. Although this opinion is probable, Sanchez regards as more probable the opinion which he embraced in his treatise on Matrimony, namely, that it is sufficient that one reside in the place with the intention of remaining the greater part of the year: "*Satis esse si ibi habitat cum animo permanendi majore anni parte.*"[54]

Finally, in the opinion of Sanchez, a quasi-domicile makes one a parishioner or diocesan for all things except the Sacrament of Orders.[55] For this latter a domicile is required. The only difference between

---

[52] Cf. p. 77.

[53] Sanchez, *Opus Morale*, lib. IV, c. 37, n. 23 ff.

[54] Sanchez, *o. c.*, n. 27.

[55] Sanchez, *De Matrimonio*, III, 23, 7.

the domicile and the quasi-domicile was that the former required an intention of permanent residence, the latter an intention of remaining for the greater part of the year.

Although the theory of Sanchez in regard to the domicile was destined finally to prevail, that institution was to unfold a future history so rambling and confusing that to call it checkered is to describe it weakly. Had Sanchez' theory been officially accepted much trouble and confusion would have been avoided in the years which followed. But it seemed that as star differs from star in glory, so also did canonists differ in their conception of quasi-domicile.

Opposition to the view of Sanchez was not long in coming. Suarez,[56] a contemporary of Sanchez, though offering a theory of quasi-domicile akin to that of Sanchez in many respects, parts company with him on the duration of the residence necessary to constitute a quasi-domicile.

Suarez admits that the greater part of a year is certainly sufficient.[57] But is it necessary? Suarez does not think so. Following and alleging Navarrus, Suarez states that it is enough to come to a place with the intention of residing there for an uncertain length of time—a notable period of time, but not the greater part of a year.[58] It may be remarked here that Suarez is the first of a series of canonists, appearing at regular intervals, who are disappointedly vague in the expression of their theories.[59]

---

[56] Suarez, lib. II, *de diebus festis*, c. XIV; t. II *de religione*, tract. de voto, lib. VI, c. 11, n. 11; *de ministro confessionis*, disp. XXV, sect. II, dub. 2, n. 5.

[57] Suarez, lib. II, *de diebus festis*, c. XIV, n. 6.

[58] Suarez, *l. c.*

[59] Especially Laymann and Fagnanus.

The view of Sanchez, however, even during his own time, did not lack defenders. Among others, Gutierrez,[60] Lessius,[61] Bonacina,[62] and Castrapalao[63] accepted the view of Sanchez in its entirety. Castrapalao[64] alone uses the word quasi-domicile. The others use the expression *domicilium paroeciale.*[65]

The opinion of Navarrus, which Suarez had already accepted, was adopted also by Paul Laymann (1635). Seeking to determine the subjects of ecclesiastical laws, Laymann declared that those who reside in a place with the intention of staying a long time, and therefore acquire a quasi-domicile, are bound by all the laws and customs in force there.[66]

In discussing the length of time one must intend to reside in a place in order to acquire a quasi-domicile, Laymann refers to the opinion of Sanchez, but accepts that of Navarrus, viz., that even those who reside in a place with the intention of remaining a shorter time than Sanchez requires, may be regarded as inhabitants.[67] Laymann calls the possessor of a quasi-domicile a quasi incola.[68] The difficulty with the view of Laymann is that, at least for practical purposes, it was too indefinite. Aside from this, Laymann has given the most precise exposition of the constitutive elements of quasi-domicile of any writer up to his time. To acquire a quasi-domicile both *animus*

---

[60] *De Matr.* cap. 63, n. 19ff.
[61] *De justit. et de jure*, lib. II, c. 40, dub. 18, n. 121.
[62] *De Matr.* q. 11, punct. 8, n. 1 ff.
[63] *De Sponsal.*, Disp. II, punct. 13, 9, n. 8 ff.
[64] *L. c.*
[65] Gutierrez, *l. c.;* Lessius, *l. c.;* Bonacina, *l. c.*
[66] Laymann, *Theologia Moralis*, lib. I, tr. IV, de legibus, c. 12.
[67] *O. c.*, lib. V, tr. VI, c. 10, n. 5.
[68] *L. c.*, n. 6.

and *factum* were necessary. The *animus* consisted in the intention to remain, the *factum* consisted in actual habitation. As soon as one came to a place with the intention of remaining, he acquired a quasi-domicile. Finally, the quasi-domicile was lost in the same way in which it was constituted, viz., not by sole intention of departing, but by an accompanying actual departure.[69]

Emanuel Gonzales Tellez, who flourished about the middle of the seventeenth century, adopted the theory of Sanchez.[70] Tellez does not mention the name quasi-domicile, using instead the expression *domicilium matrimoniale.*[71] His meaning, however, is unmistakable, as he requires for this "domicile" a residence with the intention of remaining the greater part of a year.[72]

Prosper Fagnani, the great canonist of the late seventeenth century, presented an entirely different theory of quasi-domicile. Although Fagnani uses the expression *simplex habitatio* instead of quasi-domicile, it cannot be doubted that he is speaking of what the canonists generally called quasi-domicile.[73] In his effort to determine how a person became a parishioner in a certain parish, Fagnani relates and discusses the two prevalent opinions, namely, the one that requires a domicile, the other that requires residence for the greater part of the year.[74] Fagnani rejects both theories on the plea that the chapter

---

[69] Laymann, *l. c.*

[70] Tellez, *Commentaria in Decretal.*, lib. IV, tit. III, n. 8.

[71] Tellez, *l. c.*

[72] Tellez, *l. c.*

[73] *Comm. in Decret.*, lib. III, tit. 29, n. 18, 27.

[74] *O. c.*, n. 20.

"*Is qui,*" on which, he claims, both theories are principally based, requires neither domicile nor residence for the greater part of a year.[75]

The theory of Federicus de Senis is then brought up for consideration. According to this view, a person acquires parochial rights by sole residence in a place, provided he has not come "*causa recreationis,*" or for some other passing reason, intending to return almost immediately to his domicile.[76] This theory Fagnani accepts as the truer one.[77]

Just what this canonist required for the acquisition of parochial rights is not quite clear. According to some writers,[78] Fagnani taught that one acquired parochial rights in a place provided he did not come there with the positive intention of merely passing through. Feije,[79] on the other hand, declared that while Fagnani did not require residence for the greater part of a year, neither was he content with a shorter residence, merely materially viewed and independent of every circumstance. Feije also remarks that nowhere does Fagnani even mention the necessity of intention.[80] Whatever of this, the theory of Fagnani was sufficiently vague and indefinite to render it unsatisfactory.

Despite Fagnani's rejection of the theory of Sanchez, the latter's theory found great favor with a number of the great canonists of the late seventeenth and

---

[75] *O. c.*, n. 24.

[76] *O. c.*, n. 28.

[77] *O. c.*, n. 31.

[78] Fourneret, *Le Domicile Matrimonial*, p. 116; Farren, *Domicile and Quasi-domicile*, p. 53.

[79] *De Imped. et dispensat. Matrim.*, n. 216.

[80] Feije, *l. c.*

early eighteenth centuries, including Pirhing,[81] Reiffenstuel,[82] La Croix,[83] Laurenius,[84] Schmier,[85] and Schmalzgrueber.[86] Their teaching is very definite. That of Pirhing is typical of the others: "To acquire a domicile, besides actual residence one must have the intention of remaining in the place, not always, but for a year or for the greater part of a year."[87]

The next great figure in the history of quasi-domicile is Benedict XIV (Prospero Lambertini). Nowhere, perhaps, is the unsettled and confused state of the quasi-domicile more clearly reflected than in the writings of this great canonist, prelate and Pope. This great ecclesiastic had been in turn Secretary of the Congregation of the Council, Archbishop of Bologna, and Pope. During the course of his career in each of the above ecclesiastical offices he had to deal with the problems connected with quasi-domicile, particularly in regard to the question of assistance at marriages. By reason of his great experience, one would expect from Benedict XIV precise and almost definitive information on the subject. That such was not forthcoming is an indication of the unsettled state in which, even at this late date, the quasi-domicile found itself.

In a resolution of the Sacred Congregation of the Council given in 1720,[88] when Benedict XIV was Secretary of the Congregation, and published in his

[81] Lib. II, tit. II, n. 18.
[82] Lib. II, tit. II, n. 2 ff.
[83] *Theologia Moralis*, lib. VI, p. III, n. 721.
[84] *Jus Canonicum*, lib. IV, tit. III, q. 14.
[85] *Jurisprudentia Canonico-Civilis*, lib. II, tr. I, c. 3, sect. 2, n. 26.
[86] Lib. IV, tit. III, n. 149–150.
[87] Pirhing, lib. II, tit. II, n. 18.
[88] S.C.C., in Jardren.—*Thesaurus Resolut. S.C.C.*, I, p. 351 ff.

Quaestiones Canonicae,[89] one finds the clear and unequivocal statement: "A quasi-domicile is not acquired unless one has the intention of remaining for the greater part of a year." As authorities for this teaching the names of Sanchez, Lessius, Pirhing, and Reiffenstuel are alleged.[90]

In his *Institutiones Ecclesiasticae,* written when he was Archbishop of Bologna, Benedict XIV has very little directly bearing on the theory of quasi-domicile.[91] He limits himself to the solution of practical cases, and lays down norms that must be observed in his diocese, regarding assistance at the marriages of certain classes of people, e.g., students, servants.[92]

The final utterance of Benedict XIV on the question of quasi-domicile is contained in the Constitution "*Paucis abhinc*"[93] issued by him in 1758. This Constitution was an official reply to the Archbishop of Goa who had requested information and a decision in regard to the marriages of some of his subjects. The important part of the Constitution is that wherein Benedict XIV declared—following the accepted teaching—that in order to validly contract marriage in a place, it was necessary that at least one of the parties have there a domicile or a quasi-domicile.[94] In connection with the quasi-domicile, Benedict declares: "In this matter, no other reply can be given than that, before the marriage is con-

---

[89] *Quaest. Canon.* q. 182.

[90] S.C.C. in Jardren.—*Thesaurus Resolut. S.C.C.*, I, p. 354.

[91] *Inst. Eccl.* Inst. 33, 88.

[92] *Inst. Eccl., l. c.*

[93] Const. "*Paucis abhinc,*"—*Fontes* n. 447.

[94] §5, *Fontes*, n. 447.

tracted, one of the parties should have lived in the place for at least a month."[95] In proof of this a case mentioned by Fagnani is recalled: A man and a woman, fearing interference on the part of their parents, betook themselves to a nearby town and, after residing there a while, contracted marriage. The Congregation of the Council, consulted on the point, was of the opinion that if the parties had stayed in the place of marriage for at least one month, a decision was to be given in favor of the validity of the marriage.[96] "It is doubtful," Benedict continues, "whether, in order to acquire a quasi-domicile, a residence preceding the marriage alone is required, or whether subsequent residence for some time is also necessary."[97] Benedict observes that many canonists regarded subsequent habitation as a proof of great value in determining whether or not a quasi-domicile had been acquired. However, the Congregation of the Council had decreed nothing concerning this, and, for his own part, Benedict was unwilling to add anything new in the matter.[98]

It need hardly be stated that the teaching of Benedict XIV did not help matters. Indeed, his last utterance served only to increase the obscurity surrounding the quasi-domicile. The month's residence, destined to play an important role in this matter, caused a sharp difference of opinion. Some canonists,[99] alleging the authority of the Constitution

---

[95] §7, *Fontes*, n. 447.

[96] *Fontes*, *l. c.*

[97] *Fontes*, *l. c.*

[98] *Fontes*, *l. c.*

[99] Bangen, *De Spons. et Matr.*, lib. II, 14; Van de Burgt, *De Matr.*, n. 235; Moulart, *De Sepult. et Coem.*, p. 184.

"*Paucis abhinc*," declared that residence of a month was sufficient to constitute a quasi-domicile.

Other canonists,[100] regarded it merely as a proof—a presumption that a quasi-domicile was acquired. It seems quite certain that the latter interpretation is the correct one. Benedict had stated that he was unwilling to decide the question as to whether, besides the previous residence of a month, subsequent residence in the place was also necessary. But, if Benedict had declared that a month's residence was sufficient to constitute a quasi-domicile, by that very fact he would have determined that subsequent habitation was unnecessary. Unless one wish to accuse the great canonist of being obviously illogical, one must reject the opinion of those who declared that a month's residence was sufficient to constitute a quasi-domicile.[101]

It would be useless to enter into a detailed discussion of the canonists who wrote after Benedict XIV. Each of the various and contradictory opinions already mentioned had its own champions during this time.[102] In addition, the decrees of many provincial synods, laying down the conditions necessary to acquire parochial rights for marriage, served to add to the prevailing confusion. No mention was made of intention. Actual residence for a certain period

---

[100] Gury, *Theol. Moral.*, II, n. 846: Feije, *De Imp. et Disp. Matr.*, n. 225; Bouvier, *Inst. Theol.*, IV, p. 357: Vecchiotti, *Institutiones Canonicae*, cap. XIII, 106. Farren, *o. c.*, p. 58; Zitelli, *Apparatus Juris Eccl.*, p. 421 in regard to Const. "*Paucis abhinc*," says: "Mensis igitur adjicitur ad presumptionem non ad terminum"; Aichner, *Compendium Juris Eccl.*, 164.

[101] Cf. Vechiotti, *l. c.*

[102] Cf. Wernz, Votum—*Anal. Eccl.*, vol. VII, p. 66; Feije, o. c. n. 209 ff.; Laurin, "Wesen und Bedeutung des Domicils," *A. f. k. K.*, t. 26, p. 197 ff.

was sufficient. Thus the Councils of Rheims (1849),[103] of Rouen (1850),[104] and of Sens (1850),[105] required a residence of six months. The Councils of Bourges (1850),[106] and of Auch (1851),[107] were satisfied with residence of one month.

Concluding this period, it might be mentioned that at this time the opinion of Sanchez was the generally accepted one.[108]

§2. *From the Decree of 1867 to the Code*

Up to this time Canonists had alleged texts from the Roman law [109] and chapters from the Decretals [110] in support of their various opinions. It is clear, however, from the history of quasi-domicile that none of these texts or chapters was endowed with that official decisiveness that would characterize the opinion supported by them as the only true one. It is clear also that some official declaration was sorely needed to lift the institution of quasi-domicile from the maze and confusion that had shrouded it from the beginning of its history, and to definitively determine the conditions necessary for its acquisition.

On June 7, 1867, the long awaited decree, issued by the Congregation of the Inquisition,[111] appeared, setting forth the true notion of quasi-domicile.

---

[103] *Collectio Lacensis*, IV, 126-127.
[104] *Coll. Lac.*, IV, 531.
[105] *Coll. Lac.*, IV, 894.
[106] *Coll. Lac.*, IV, 1118-9.
[107] *Coll. Lac.*, vol. IV, col. 1191.
[108] Cf. Wernz, Votum in *Anal. Eccl.*, vol. VII, p. 66; Feije *l. c.*
[109] C. III, 24. 2.
[110] C. 3, *de sepult.*, III, 12 in VI°; c. 10, X, *de sepult.*, III, 28; c. 46, C. XVI, q. 1.
[111] *Collectanea S. C. de Prop. Fide*, n. 1407.

This decree, sent to the Bishops of England and the United States of America, contained the following regulations:

1°. To constitute a quasi-domicile two conditions are simultaneously required, viz., residence in a place and the intention of remaining there the greater part of a year.[112]

2°. From the very first day that the two conditions are simultaneously verified—namely the intention and the actual residence—it is to be judged that a quasi-domicile has been acquired.

3°. If it is not clearly evident that the above mentioned intention is present, recourse must be had to such indications as beget moral certitude.

4°. The month's residence, mentioned by *Benedict* XIV, is to be taken as a *presumptio juris* that the requisite intention is present, and hence that a quasi-domicile has been acquired. This presumption is destroyed by contrary proof.[113]

Any doubt as to the value of this Instruction was removed by an answer of the Holy Office to a query of the Bishops of Ireland assembled at Maynooth, Ireland, in 1875.[114] The Bishops had asked if they might "safely hold and apply in practice the opinion of those who maintained that one month's residence in a place is sufficient in order to validly contract marriage there." The reply of the Holy Office was that the proper priest for assistance at marriage was the parish priest of domicile or quasi-domicile. To determine how the quasi-domicile was acquired,

---

[112] *Coll. S. C. de Prop. Fide., l. c.:* "ad constituendum vero quasi-domicilium . . . duo haec simul requiruntur, habitatio nempe in eo loco ubi matrimonium contrabitur, atque animus ibidem permanendi per majorem anni partem."

[113] *Collect. S. C. de Prop. Fide, l. c.*

[114] Cf. Farren, p. 62.

the Bishops should consult the rule laid down in the instruction of 1867.[115]

Wernz and Pius a Langonio, two eminent canonists whose *vota* [116] were favorably received by the Congregation of the Council, were very clear and definite in their opinions concerning the value of the decree of 1867.

According to Wernz,[117] the canonical doctrine proposed in the decree was to be regarded as absolutely certain, not only in theory but in practice. "According to this doctrine," he continues, "not only were marriages declared null, but after a declaration of nullity new marriages were permitted. This could not be done, unless this doctrine were entirely certain."[118]

According to Langonio, the decree was to be considered not as a law properly speaking, but as a directive norm in which the authentic notion of quasi-domicile was handed down, and to which must be granted the force of law.[119]

It is then with some surprise that one notices some canonists clinging to the old erroneous views. Thus, Lehmkuhl [120] was of the opinion that a quasi-domicile could be acquired by residence for a notable part of a year. He regarded four months as a notable part. According to Ballerini-Palmieri [121] residence for "some

---

[115] Farren, *l. c.*

[116] Wernz, Votum—*Anal. Eccl.*, vol. VII, p. 62 ff.; Langonio, Votum —*Anal. Eccl.*, vol. XIII, p. 339 ff.

[117] Wernz, Votum,—*Anal. Eccl.*, vol. VII, p. 68.

[118] Wernz, Votum, *l. c.*

[119] Langonio, Votum,—*Anal. Eccl.* vol. XIII, p. 344.

[120] Lehmkuhl, *Theologia Moralis*, II, n. 775.

[121] Ballerini-Palmieri, *Opus Theologicum Morale*, vol. VI, tr. 10, sect. 8, n. 1186.

months" was sufficient. Finally Lombardi[122] required a notable part of a year, without defining what he meant by the expression "notable part."

None of these opinions, however, had any foundation. Each alike was opposed to the clear wording of the Instruction of the Holy Office, to the almost unanimous consent of Canonists,[123] and to the constant and frequent teaching of the Roman Congregations.[124]

The general and certain rule, then, that prevailed after 1867, required for the acquisition of a quasi-domicile: residence with the intention of remaining the greater part of a year.[125]

While the Instruction of the Holy Office definitely determined the law in regard to the acquisition of a quasi-domicile, it afforded no certain solution for the practical difficulties that were continually arising, especially in connection with the intention of remaining. As a result, the authorities of not a few nations and dioceses sought some modification of the law in order to overcome these difficulties. The Holy See acceded to their requests and a number of Concessions were granted.

---

[122] Lombardi, *Inst. Juris Canonici Privati*, III, p. 187.

[123] Gasparri, *de Matr.*, n. 916; Wernz, *Jus Decretalium*, IV, n. 177; Lega, *De Judiciis*, I, n. 336; Ojetti, *Synopsis Rerum Moralium*, n. 1881; D'Annibale, *Summula* I, §84.

[124] S. C. C., *Nullit. Matr.* 18 Sept. 1878—*A.S.S.*, XI, (1878), p. 566; S.C.C., *Nullit. Matr.* 12 Dec. 1885—*A.S.S.*, XVIII, 493; S.C.C., *Parisien*, 14 Dec. 1889—*A.S.S.*, XXII 498; S.C.C., *Parisien* 6 March 1907,—*Anal. Eccl.* XV, 237 ff.; S.R.R., *in Ravennaten.*, 29 Dec. 1911—*A.A.S.*, IV, (1912), 328 ff.; S.R.R., *in Vladislavien.*, 7 Dec. 1912—*Decisiones Coram Lega*, p. 349; S.R.R., *Parisien*, 22 April 1913—*Decis. S.R.Rotae*, Vol. V, dec. XXIII, n. 7; S.R.R., *Parisien*, 24 April 1914—A.A.S., VI, (1914), 409 ff.

[125] Gasparri, *de Matr.* n. 916; Wernz, Votum—*Anal. Eccl.*, Vol. VII, p. 68.

The first of these was granted to the Bishops of the United States in 1886. The Holy Office, in a letter dated May 16, 1886, decreed "that those passing from a place where the '*Tametsi*' was in force to another place, are to be considered to have a quasi-domicile there, if they have remained there for a month, without enquiry being made regarding their intention of remaining the greater part of the year."[126]

The Holy Office made a second concession, when in 1898, it granted to the Archbishop of Paris a privilege, the same in every detail as the American concession, with the exception that a residence of six months was required instead of one month.[127]

In 1903, the Archbishop of Paris requested the Holy See to extend to his diocese the American privilege of the month's residence. This was done by a decree of the Sacred Congregation of the Council on May 20, 1905.[128]

Doubt soon arose as to the exact import and scope of the American and the original Paris concessions.

In regard to the American concession, it was quite certain that the decree of the Holy Office did not regard the month's residence as a "*presumptio juris tantum.*" This had already been determined in the Instruction of 1867. Further than this, however, canonists did not agree. Some authorities, including Gasparri [129] and Lega,[130] were of the opinion that by sole residence for a month one acquired a quasi-domicile.

---

[126] *Collectanea S. C. de Prop. Fide*, n. 1413.

[127] *A.S.S.*, XXXI, 404.

[128] *A.S.S.*, XXXVIII, 208 ff.

[129] *De Matrimonio*, n. 916.

[130] Lega, *De Judiciis Eccl.* I, n. 338 nota 1.

Others [131] again, declared that residence for a month gave rise to a "*presumptio juris et de jure,*" nothing more. By way of comment, it may be mentioned that the officials of the Roman Rota, in deciding a recent matrimonial case, clearly favored the latter opinion.[132]

Arguing from the Paris concession, Noldin [133] and others [134] declared that a merely material residence of six months was sufficient to constitute a quasi-domicile. Roman authorities, however, had no sympathy with this view. The Assessor of the Holy Office, in a note to the response to the Archbishop of Paris (1898), declared that the Sacred Congregation did not wish to settle the question, as to whether or not a merely material residence of six months was sufficient to constitute a quasi-domicile. The Paris concession was a favor granted to that city, and was not to be applied to any other place.[135]

The Assessor of the Holy Office, requested by the Congregation of the Council to expose the mind of the Holy Office on the six months residence replied, "In this Supreme Tribunal, it has never been adopted as a general principle, that those who have resided six months in a parish can validly contract marriage without making any enquiries concerning the intention

[131] Boudinhon, "Quelques reflexions sur le domicile"—*Canoniste Contemporain,* XXII (1899) p. 273; *Collationes Brugenses,* V (1900) p. 306.

[132] S. R. R. *in Causa Parisien* 24 April 1914—*A.A.S.*, VI (1914), 410. "Jus enim in favorem matrimonii ex facto commorationis induxit praesumptionem intentionis . . . presumptionem vero juris et de jure ex commoratione per spatium unius mensis pro U. S."

[133] Noldin, *Theologia Moralis,* I, p. 148, nota 2 (ed. 4º).

[134] Van den Berghe, *De Legibus,* n. 107; Collationes Brugenses, IV (1899) p. 184; cf. Alberti, p. 7, nota 1.

[135] Wernz, *Jus Decretalium,* IV, n. 139, nota 27; *Il Monitore Ecclesiastico,* Vol. X, p. II, p. 221.

of remaining. The dispositions granted for a certain Paris case must be regarded as entirely particular ones."[136]

Finally, this opinion of Noldin was openly reproved by the Officials of the Rota in a Ravenna case decided in 1911.[137]

Whatever the mind of the Holy See regarding these concessions, this much may be said of them, viz., that they marked the beginning of a twofold evolution whose final stage was reached in the New Code of Canon Law.[138]

By a strange quirk of fate, the quasi-domicile, which had received its greatest development in connection with the Sacrament of Matrimony, was erased from the matrimonial legislation by the decree *Ne Temere*, and the month's residence was substituted in its place. The quasi-domicile, however, retained all its importance in other ecclesiastical matters, and here it may not be amiss to say that, with the exception of the *episcopus proprius* for the reception of Orders, it produced the same effects in Canon law as did the domicile.[139]

Such was the historical development of quasi-domicile in Canon law. Though attended throughout its whole history with misunderstanding and confusion, it was, nevertheless, a very reasonable institution, and one admirably suited to the mobility of the modern world. Its weak point was the intention,

---

[136] *A.S.S.*, XXXVIII, 208 ff.

[137] S.R.R. *Causa Ravennaten.*, 29 Dec. 1911—*A.A.S.*, IV, (1912), 328 ff.

[138] Cf. Canon 92, §2 and Canon 1097 §1, n. 2.

[139] Sanchez, *de Matr.*, III, 22, 7; D'Angelo, *Il domicilio ecclesiastico*, p. 40 ff.; Alberti, p. 13 ff.

and it was this that had caused the majority of the difficulties that arose, especially in connection with the validity of marriages. Some change was required to increase the efficiency of this institution. This change was effected by the Code.[140]

[140] Canon 92, §2. "Quasi-domicilium acquiritur commoratione . . . protracta ad majorem anni partem."

PART II—PRESENT LEGISLATION

DOMICILE AND QUASI-DOMICILE IN THE NEW CODE

INTRODUCTION

The Code of Canon law marks the final stage in the development of the notions of domicile and quasi-domicile. From the preceding historical sketch, it is clear that these two institutions, particularly the quasi-domicile, had evolved to a great extent. It cannot be denied however, that no little doubt and confusion concerning them, with consequent practical difficulties, existed even up to the eve of the Code. This is not to be wondered at when all things are considered. In the first place, the legislator had never issued an official declaration clearly setting forth a complete canonical theory of domicile or quasi-domicile, until the Holy Office Instruction of 1867.[1] This Instruction, as we have seen, did not entirely do away with old erroneous views; and subsequent particular replies served only to multiply difficulties.[2] Secondly, the intention, the formal element of domicile and quasi-domicile, was a *quid internum*, not directly perceptible. It was, therefore, difficult to prove in the external forum and calculated

[1] S.C.S. Off., litt. encycl., 7 June 1867—*Collect. S.C. de Prop. Fide*, n. 1303.

[2] Cf. page 90-91

to give rise to innumerable doubts and practical difficulties. Finally, domicile and quasi-domicile had to meet different requirements; and for the different cases, different rules were adopted. Thus, to determine the proper Bishop for the reception of Orders an entirely special domicile was required.[3] In this connection also, although the domicile was commonly thought to be attached to a parish, many eminent authorities acknowledged a purely diocesan domicile.[4]

Evidently there was ample room for clearer and more definite teaching concerning domicile and quasi-domicile. Indeed, many great canonists [5] openly expressed the desire that the ecclesiastical authority perfect and modify the canonical doctrine on domicile and quasi-domicile, and accommodate it to present day conditions and circumstances. With the publication of the Code their fondest hopes were realized, and, although some matters in connection with domicile and quasi-domicile are not beyond dispute, a good many hitherto doubtful points have been definitively settled, and a number of useful changes have been introduced.

The present legislation is contained in canons 90 to 95, forming part of a preliminary section to the second book of the Code. This arrangement is not without some significance. For, in the new canon law it would appear that it is in the mind of the legislator

---

[3] Cf. Innocent XII, Const. "*Speculatores,*" 4 Nov. 1694—*Fontes* n. 258; Gasparri, *De Ordinatione*, n. 830 ff.

[4] Gennari, *Quistioni Canoniche*, q. 211; D'Angelo, *Il domicilio ecclesiastico*, p. 109. Cf. above p. 62 ff.

[5] Gasparri, *De Matrimonio*, n. 1089; Langonio, Votum—*Anal. Eccl.*, vol. XIII (1905) p. 453 ff.; De Becker, *De Spons, et Matr.*, p. 95.

to include domicile and quasi-domicile among those general attributes or notes which affect a person's juridical capacity in general in connection with the exercise of his christian rights and duties. Following the generally accepted method, the place of origin will be considered before discussing the domicile and quasi-domicile.

CHAPTER IV

THE PLACE OF ORIGIN

The New Code has sounded the deathknell of the troublesome and confusing domicile of origin. In the new legislation, by birth (*origo—nativitas*) one secures, not a *domicilium originis*, but a *locus originis*—a place of origin.[1] The new law is eminently clear on the point; and so, the domicile of origin passes from canonical history. Although the *origo* is still retained in canon law, our law in this respect differs greatly from the Roman law. In Roman law by birth (*origo*) one acquired citizenship in a local community or city, with all the legal effects such a status naturally entails.[2] In canon law by birth one acquires a place of origin, which is important, and that very slightly, only in regard to the proper bishop for the reception of orders.[3] The *origo*, then, is of very little practical moment in canon law. Its importance now is chiefly archeological: it is a keepsake, a relic, of a once famous legal institution.

Canon 90, §1.—Locus originis filii, etiam neophyti, est ille in quo, cum filius natus est, domicilium, aut, in defectu domicilii, quasi-domicilium habebat pater vel, si filius sit illegitimus aut postumus, mater.

---

[1] Canon 90.

[2] D. L. 1. 1. pr.; C. X. 40 (39). 7.

[3] Canon 956. Cf. Ojetti, *Commentarium*, II, 36; Vidal, *Jus Canonicum* II, n. 7; Chelodi, *Jus de Personis*, n. 92; Maroto, *Institutiones Juris Canonici*, I, n. 408; Badii, *Institutiones juris canonici*, I, 82.

§2. Si agatur de filio vagorum, locus originis est ipsemet nativitatis locus; si de exposito, est locus in quo inventus fuit.

Before the Code it was the common and certain teaching of canonists,[4] confirmed by ecclesiastical authority,[5] that one's place of origin was the place in which, at the time of birth, one's father had his domicile, regardless of whether the birth took place there or elsewhere.[6] This teaching, not, however, without some change, viz., in regard to quasi-domicile, has been adopted by the New Code.

Canon 90 defines the *locus originis* as the place in which the father had a domicile, or, in defect of domicile, a quasi-domicile at the time of the child's birth. The *locus originis*, then, is not that place in which one is actually or naturally born; but it is the place where, according to the law, one should have been born, i.e., in the place where the father had his domicile. It is the legal, not the actual place of birth, that determines one's place of origin.[7] Thus if it should happen that a child be born in some place where his parents are staying for a short time, outside of their domicile, by a fiction of law the child is considered to have been born in the place of his father's

---

[4] Sanchez, *De Matrimonio*, III, 23, 3; Honorante, *Praxis Secretariae Tribunalis*, C. 1, nota 9: Schmalzgrueber, lib. II, tit. II, n. 21; D'Annibale, *Summula*, I, §82; Alberti, *De domicilio ecclesiastico*, n. 2; D'Angelo, *Il domicilio ecclesiastico*, p. 21.

[5] Innocent XII, Const. "*Speculatores*," n. 5 *Fontes*, 258.

[6] Honorante, *Praxis Secretariae Tribunalis*, c. 1. nota 9; Gasparri, *De Ordinatione*, n. 808; Many, *De Ordinatione*, n. 29.

[7] Ojetti, *Commentarium*, II, p. 37; Vidal, *Jus Canonicum*, II, n. 8; Chelodi, *Jus de Personis*, n. 92. "Locus originis ille est in quo juridice nati sumus; quod de facto sed fortuito alibi, rem non mutat."

domicile.[8] The reason for this fiction seems to be the desire of the legislator to avoid the difficulties which would arise in determining the place of origin, when the child is born "*ex accidenti*," i.e., while his parents are away from their domicile.

The Code has introduced an innovation in regard to the effect of the quasi-domicile on the place of origin. Before the Code, quasi-domicile was an entirely unimportant factor in the determination of the place of origin.[9] In the new legislation, the quasi-domicile, is sufficient, in the absence of domicile, to determine the place of origin.[10] It must be remembered that the quasi-domicile obtains this effect, only *in defectu domicilii*. Therefore, even though the child be born in the place where his father had a quasi-domicile, if at the same time the father had a domicile, it is the domicile of the father, not the quasi-domicile, which determines the *locus originis*.[11]

Can the *locus originis* be manifold? If the father has a domicile in two places, has the child a *locus originis* in each? Before the Code a sharp controversy existed on this point. The matter on which the controversy turned was in connection with the proper bishop for the reception of Orders, by reason of

---

[8] D. L. 1. 6. Schmalzgrueber, lib. I, tit. XI, n. 37; Gasparri, *De ordinatione*, n. 816; Many, *De Ordinatione*, n. 22; Alberti, *De domicilio ecclesiastico*, n. 22; Ojetti, *Commentarium*, II, p. 37. "Non refert, quod quis natus fuerit alibi, quia v. gr., parentes ejus extra locum domicilii sui, dum ipse nascebatur, versabantur . . . nam adhuc fictione juris in loco domicilii patris natus censetur."

[9] Alberti, *De domicilio ecclesiastico*, n. 2; D'Angelo, *Il domicilio ecclesiastico*, p. 21.

[10] Canon 90, §1.

[11] Vidal, *Jus Canonicum*, II, n. 8; Maroto, *Institutiones Juris Canonici*, I, n. 407, nota 3; Bouuaert-Simenon, *Manuale Juris Canonici*, n. 240; Muniz, *Derecho Parroquial*, I, n. 76.

origin. Although the difference of opinion existed before the publication of the Constitution "*Speculatores*,"[12] it was not until after the appearance of this Constitution that the question was seriously discussed.[13] Many more recent canonists, including Gasparri [14] and Many,[15] held that the proper bishop by reason of origin was essentially one. According to these writers, a twofold place of origin cannot be sustained under the Constitution "*Speculatores*." Other prominent authorities, including St. Alphonsus,[16] and Ballerini,[17] declared that there could be two bishops of origin. The case that both sides considered was that regarding the "accidental" birth of a child whose father had two domiciles, i.e., the child was born in some place other than either of the places in which the father had his two domiciles.

According to Gasparri,[18] in this case the *locus originis* of the child is in the placc of that domicile in which the father was actually dwelling at the time of the birth of the child, the reason being that by a fiction of law the wife, even though absent, is considered to be with her husband.[19] If at the time of birth, the father was not dwelling in either of his two domiciles, then the *locus originis* is the place of that domicile from which the mother last departed.[20]

---

[12] Innocent XII, Const. "*Speculatores*," 4 Nov. 1694. Cf. Barbosa, *De off. et potest. Epis.*, alleg. IV, n. 4 ff; Pirhing, lib. I, tit. XI, n. 31; Passerini, *Commentarium in Sexto*, c. cum nullus, n. 16 ff.

[13] Riganti, *Comm. in Reg. Apost. Cancell.* in Reg. 24, §III, n. 8 ff.

[14] *De Ordinatione*, n. 819.

[15] *De Ordinatione*, n. 29.

[16] *Theologia Moralis*, lib. VI, tr. V, C. 2, n. 773.

[17] *Opus Theologicum Morale*, V, tract. de ordine, n. 61.

[18] *L. c.*

[19] 1. Hujusmodi, Legatum, ff., De legatis.

[20] Gasparri, *l. c.;* Many, *l. c.*

On the other hand, St. Alphonsus and Ballerini argued that the child had a *locus originis* in the two places where his father had a domicile. There was no reason, according to them, why one place should be preferred to the other.[21] Strangely enough these canonists did not discuss the case of a child born in the place of one of his father's domiciles. Whether or not it was taken for granted that the domicile in which the child was born determined his place of origin is not clear. Thus matters stood up to the New Code.

Canon 90 has not, at least explicitly, settled this question. It would seem, however, that the notion of the place of origin, as handed down by the Code, does not exclude the possibility of a twofold place of origin. In canon 90 it is declared that the *locus originis* is determined by the father's domicile. If the father has two domiciles there seems to be no reason why the child cannot have two places of origin. It is not as if the *locus originis* corresponded to the truth, i.e., to the actual place of birth. On the contrary, the place of origin is a legal fiction.[22] Besides the fact that it is not excluded by the law, the opinion affirming the possibility of a twofold place of origin, has found unanimous favor among the commentators on the New Code, enlisting the authority of such eminent canonists as Vidal, Vermeersch-Creusen, Coronata, Toso, Muniz, Cocchi, Woywod, and Bouuaert-Simenon.[23] In the

---

[21] St. Alphonsus, *l. c.;* Ballerini, *l. c.*

[22] Vidal, *Jus Canonicum,* II, n. 7; Toso, *Commentaria,* lib. II, p. 17.

[23] Vidal, *Jus Canonicum,* II, n. 7; Vermeersch-Creusen, *Epitome juris canonici,* I, n. 181; Coronata, *Institutiones juris canonici,* I, n. 123; Toso, *Commentaria,* lib. II, p. 17; Muniz, *Derecho Parroquial,*

light of this, it is clear that the opinion admitting the possibility of a twofold place of origin must be regarded as certain and more common. In practice, if particular law does not declare otherwise, it would seem that, in the exercise of rights, an individual could choose whatever of the two places of origin he prefers.[24]

As in the preceding legislation,[25] the place of origin of illegitimate or posthumous children is determined by the domicile or quasi-domicile of the mother.[26] This regulation in regard to illegitimate children obtains, even in the case in which the father is certainly known and his domicile is different from that of the mother. The reason for this regulation is that although the father is naturally known, he is not recognized by law as the father. He is, in a word, juridically unknown.[27] It is to be noted that the general rule in regard to illegitimate children is modified in the case of children legitimated by a subsequent marriage.[28] Canon 1117 is decisive on the point. "Children legitimated by a subsequent marriage, as far as canonical effects are concerned, are placed in the same position as legitimate children, unless the opposite is expressly stated." There is no express provision to the contrary in the

t. 1, n. 76; Cocchi, *Commentarium*, II, p. 19; Woywod, *Practical Commentary*, n. 67; Bouuaert-Simenon, *Manuale juris canonici*, n. 240.

[24] Toso, *l. c.*

[25] S. C. C. 15 Feb. 1704, — Soglia, *Inst. juris privati*, n. 44.

[26] Canon 90, § 1.—The determination of the place of origin by the quasi-domicile is, of course, new.

[27] D. L. l. 9; Vidal, *Jus Canonicum*, II, n. 8; Maroto, *Institutiones juris canonici*, I, n. 407; Bouuaert-Simenon, *Manuale juris canonici*, n. 240.

[28] Canon 1117.

present case, and the only conclusion is that they acquire the same place of origin as if they had been legitimate from the beginning, i.e., their father's domicile determines the place of origin.[29]

A change has been introduced by the new law[30] in regard to neophytes or converts. In the old law, as ordained by the Constitution *"Cupientes"*[31] of Paul III, which remained in force up to the Code, neophytes were considered to have their place of origin in the place where they were baptized.[32] In the present legislation, the neophyte follows the ordinary rules, i.e., his place of origin is the place in which, at the time of his birth, his father had his domicile; or in the absence of a domicile his quasi-domicile.[33]

Before the Code there does not seem to have been an unanimity of opinion regarding the *locus originis* of children whose parents were *vagi.* This much is certain. In regard to the proper bishop for Orders, the *locus originis* of a child, whose father had no domicile at the time the child was born, was considered to be in the actual place of the father's birth. This prescription was laid down in the Constitution *"Speculatores"* of Innocent XII,[34] which retained its full force up to

---

[29] Vidal, *Jus Canonicum,* II, n. 8; Bouuaert-Simenon, *Manuale juris canonici,* n. 240; Farren, *Domicile and Quasi-domicile,* p. 69.

[30] Canon 90, 1.

[31] Paul. III, Const. *"Cupientes,"* 31 March 1541—*Bullarium Romanum,* t. VI, p. 336.

[32] Gasparri, *De Ordinatione,* n. 807; D'Annibale, *Summula,* I, § 82; Many, *DeOrdinatione,* n. 31; Alberti, *De domicilio ecclesiastico,* n. 2.

[33] Canon 90, § 1. Cf. Vidal, *Jus Canonicum,* II, n. 8; Ojetti, *Commentarium,* II, p. 37.

[34] Innocent XII, Const. *"Speculatores,"* 4 Nov. 1694,—Fontes, n. 258; cf. Honorante, *Praxis Secretariae Tribunalis,* cap. I, nota 9.

the Code.[35] In other matters some authorities declared that the *locus originis* of a child whose parents were *vagi* was the place in which the child was actually born.[36] All doubt and uncertainty on this point has been removed by the Code. The new law has determined that the place of origin of a child, whose parents have no domicile or quasi-domicile at the time of birth, is the actual place of birth.[37] The question arises here: what is the *locus originis* of a child whose father is a *vagus* and whose mother, lawfully separated, has a domicile or quasi-domicile at the time of birth? It is difficult to see how a child born in these circumstances can be said to be born of parents who are *vagi;* it is also difficult, therefore, to see how the second paragraph of Canon 90 would apply, declaring the child's place of origin to be the actual place of birth. Vermeersch[38] likens a child born in these circumstances to a posthumous child and thus declares that the child secures a *locus originis* in the place of his mother's domicile or quasi-domicile. This opinion has the support of De Meester,[39] Bouuaert-Simenon,[40] Coronata,[41] and Woywod,[42] and may be regarded as truly and solidly probable.

---

[35] Cf. Gasparri, *De Ordinatione,* n. 808; Alberti, *De domicilio ecclesiastico,* n. 22.

[36] Schmalzgrueber, lib. II, tit. II, n. 2; Alberti, *De domicilio ecclesiastico,* n. 2; D'Angelo, *Il domicilio ecclesiastico,* p. 21.

[37] Canon 90, § 2. "Si agatur de filio vagorum, locus originis est ipsemet nativitatis locus." Cf. Vidal, *Jus Canonicum,* II, n. 8; Ojetti, *Commentarium,* vol. II, p. 38.

[38] Vermeersch-Creusen, *Epitome,* I, n. 181.

[39] *Juris Canonici et Juris Canonico Civilis Compendium,* I, n. 313.

[40] *Manuale juris canonici,* n. 240.

[41] *Institutiones juris canonici,* n. 123, nota 3.

[42] *Practical Commentary,* n. 67.

As in the old law,[43] so also in the new, the place of origin of foundlings (*expositi*) is declared to be the place in which they were found.[44] Before the Code the question was discussed whether or not a foundling's place of origin was changed, when at some future date his parents and their place of domicile at the time of birth became known. The common and certain, in fact the only opinion, answered in the affirmative.[45] The reason given was that if the child's parents became known, he ceased to be a foundling.[46] The Code has not explicitly adopted this regulation, but there can be no doubt that it obtains in the new legislation. The place in which the child was found merely supplies the place of the domicile or quasi-domicile of his parents. When this is discovered, the place of origin is determined by this domicile or quasi-domicile. This teaching has received the support of a great many commentators on the Code.[47]

---

[43] Honorante, *Praxis Secretariae Tribunalis*, cap. 1, nota 9; Gasparri, *De Ordinatione*, n. 826; D'Angelo, *Il domicilio ecclesiastico*, p. 21.

[44] Canon 90, § 2; Vermeersch-Creusen, *Epitome*, I, n. 181.

[45] Honorante, *Praxis Secretariae Tribunalis*, cap. 1, nota 9; Gasparri, *De Ordinatione*, n. 826; Many, *De Ordinatione*, n. 30.

[46] Honorante, *l. c.* "Ratio est quia ex quo de parentibus constat, desinit expositus esse."

[47] De Meester, *Compendium juris canonici*, I, n. 313; Vermeersch-Creusen, *Epitome*, I, n. 181; Ojetti, *Commentarium*, II, p. 38; "Sed cum, ut procedebat antiquo jureet videtur procedere etiam nunc, . . . si de parentibus constat, ii non debent amplius haberi tamquam expositi, sed ad determinandam eorum originem applicandae sunt regulae traditae in 1." Muniz, *Derecho Parroquial*, n. 76; Coronata, *Institutiones*, I, n. 123; Blat, *Commentarium*, II, n. 9; Bouuaert-Simenon, *Manuale juris canonici*, n. 240; Cocchi, *Commentarium*, II, p. 9; Woywod, *Practical Commentary*, n. 67; Ayrinhac, *General Legislation*, n. 190.

Coronata[48] is of the opinion that a twofold place of origin is to be attributed to an adopted child. According to him, besides the place of origin which one acquired at birth, the adopted child acquires also a place of origin from his adoptive father, which he retains as long as he remains in the latter's family. This opinion was defended, before the Code, by D'Annibale[49] and Alberti.[50] Other canonists take a different view of the matter.[51] Maroto,[52] for example, declares that since the Code does not touch this matter, no exception to the general rule can be admitted.

Coronata[53] then appeals to Canon 6, 4°, which declares that in doubt we must not recede from the old law. This argument, however, falls on two scores. In the first place, the law is not doubtful. On the contrary, the legislation on this point is eminently clear. The place of origin is determined by the domicile or quasi-domicile of the natural parents at the time of the child's birth. Canon 90, §1, is decisive on this point.[54] In the second place, it cannot be granted that the opinion of Coronata formed a part of the pre-Code law. It was mentioned by only two writers,[55] ignored by almost all, and enjoyed not the slightest official support. It is true that in Roman law the adopted child acquired the *origo* of his adoptive father; but the

---

[48] *Institutiones,* I, n. 123.

[49] *Summula,* I, n. 83, nota 6.

[50] *De domicilio ecclesiastico,* n. 2.

[51] Maroto, *Institutiones,* I, n. 407; Bouuaert-Simenon, *Manuale juris canonici,* n. 240; Muniz, *Derecho Parroquial,* t. 1, n. 76.

[52] *L. c.*

[53] *L. c.*

[54] Bouuaert-Simenon, *o. c.*, n. 240.

[55] D'Annibale, *Summula,* I, § 83, nota 6; Alberti, *De domicilio ecclesiastico,* n. 2.

Roman law expressly granted that.[56] Besides, our law in this respect, i.e., in regard to *origo,* is completely different from the Roman law. Finally, the place of origin is a fiction of law, and a fiction of law has a place only in cases expressly stated in the law.[57] The *locus originis* of an adopted child is not stated in the law. The conclusion is, it does not exist. It seems that the opinion of Coronata is devoid of any real probability, whether intrinsic or extrinsic.

If the true place of origin is unknown some canonists declare that the place of baptism can be regarded as the place of origin.[58] These writers arrive at this conclusion by the following argumentation. In the old law the place of baptism was received for the place of origin. From the general principles of law, as enunciated in Canon 6, 2° and 4°, it would seem that the same regulation can be applied in the new law. The argument is that of Maroto,[59] whom the other defenders of this opinion follow.

There does not seem to be the slightest foundation for the opinion of Maroto, either in the old or in the new law. In the first place, the particular prescription of the old law, to which these canonists appeal, was not made in favor of those whose place of origin was unknown. It was established as a particular privilege for converts and for them only.[60] Again, this deter-

[56] D. L. 1. 15 3.

[57] Benedict XIV, Ep. Ency. *"Ad audientiam,"* n. 15, 15 Febr. 1753 — *Fontes,* n. 424. "Fictio juris non habet locum, nisi in casibus a jure expressis."

[58] Maroto, *Institutiones,* I, n. 407; Bouuaert-Simenon, *Manuale Juris Canonici,* n. 240; Coronata, *Institutiones,* I, n. 123; Muniz, *Derecho Parroquial,* t. 1, n. 76; Chelodi, *Jus de Personis,* n. 92.

[59] *L. c.*

[60] Paul III, Const. *"Cupientes,"* 31 March 154 — *Bullarium Romanum,* t. VI, p. 336. Cf. Many, *De Ordinatione,* n. 31.

mination of the place of origin for neophytes (converts) was by a fiction of law. But one of the principal rules governing the play of the fiction of law is that it cannot be extended from person to person.[61] To extend a fiction from person to person is to induce a new fiction of law. To do this is entirely beyond the power of a private author; a fiction of law can be established only by public authority.[62]

In virtue of what has been said, it would seem that the arguments drawn from Canon 6, 2° and 4° are not conclusive. Canon 6, 2° does not apply because canon 90 certainly does not restate the former law. The reason for this is that there was no former law in connection with persons whose place of origin was unknown. The extension of the regulation made in favor of neophytes to those whose place of origin was unknown, was, as we have seen, unlawful. Canon 6, 4° does not apply because there is no doubt regarding whether or not canon 90 differs from the old law. There was no old law on the point. Finally the new legislation, in abolishing the place of baptism as a determinant of the place of origin for neophytes, implicitly condemns this view.

While extrinsic probability cannot be denied to the opinion of Maroto, it does not seem to enjoy any intrinsic probability.

---

[61] Menochius, *De Praesumptionibus,* lib. I, q. 8, n. 35. "Fictio non extenditure de persona ad personam." Reiffenstuel, lib. I, tit. II, n. 184; Roberti, *De Processibus,* II, n. 376.

[62] Benedict XIV, Ep. Ency. *"Ad Audientiam,"* n. 15, 15 Febr. 1753—*Fontes,* n. 424; Menochius, *o. c.,* n. 17. "Fictio ab homine numquam induci potest." Reiffenstuel, *l. c.; *Ojetti, *Synopsis, v.* Fictio juris, n. 2208; Roberti, *l. c.*

CHAPTER V

CONCEPT OF DOMICILE AND QUASI-DOMICILE

§1. *Definition*

The Code has not defined domicile, but has declared merely under what conditions it may be acquired. It is important, however, to give, even though briefly, some general notion and definition of this most important institution.

In general, it would seem that the essence of domicile consists in the fact of the existence in a certain place of one's permanent seat (residence—habitat—home). The phenomenon of a person dwelling in a place in which he has established himself permanently, considered from a social and economic point of view, constitutes one's home (residence), the center of one's social and business affairs. Considered from a juridical point of view, this phenomenon constitutes one's domicile, the primary effect of which is to establish a legal relation between the individual and the place of his domicile.[1] Domicile then is the legal conception of residence; and while it is admitted that residence is not domicile unless accompanied by the circumstances under which the law will recognize it, it must not be forgotten that after all that which in domicile the law does recognize is residence. From what has been said,

[1] Ojetti, *"Commentarium,"* II, p. 40.

it is clear that the domicile, *per se,* is not a fiction of law. It is not something which exists solely in the speculation of the jurist, in the world of abstractions and ideas. On the contrary it is founded upon something eminently real, material, concrete—as is the fact of having in a place one's permanent residence.

To sustain the realty of domicile, however, is not to deny the possibility or necessity of a fictitious domicile. No reality is such that a fiction cannot spring out of it. Indeed, the existence of this fictitious domicile, which both the Roman and the Canon Law admit,[2] serves to prove the reality of this institution. It is an exception to the general rule, and as the well known axiom has it, "*Exceptio firmat regulam.*"

Little need be said of the quasi-domicile. It has ever been regarded as an extension of the domicile, an attenuated domicile, a *domicilium improprium.*[3] In fact, the only difference in notion between the domicile and the quasi-domicile consists in the intention. To constitute a domicile, an intention of permanent residence is necessary; to constitute a quasi-domicile it is sufficient that one have the intention of remaining for the greater part of a year.[4]

A domicile, therefore, may now be defined as "residence in a place with the intention of remaining there always if nothing unforseen occurs." A quasi-domicile may be defined as "residence in a place with the intention of remaining the greater part of a year if nothing unforseen occurs."

---

[2] D. L., 1, 38, 3; D. L., I, 23, 1; D. L., I, 22, 3; Canon 93.

[3] Chelodi, "*Jus de Personis,*" n. 92.

[4] Cf. S. R. Rota in *Causa Ravennaten,* 15 May, 1911, *A.A.S.,* III (1911), 486.

§2. *Division*

According to the new legislation, the domicile and quasi-domicile may be divided into the voluntary and necessary domicile and quasi-domicile, and into the parochial and diocesan domicile and quasi-domicile. The voluntary domicile and quasi-domicile are acquired by an act of one's own will, whether by actual residence with the intention of remaining or by residence alone.[5] The necessary domicile and quasi-domicile are imposed by law regardless of actual circumstances.[6] The parochial domicile or quasi-domicile is that which is established in a parish or quasi-parish.[7] The diocesan domicile or quasi-domicile is that which is established in a diocese, vicariate or prefecture apostolic, but not in any parish or quasi-parish of the respective diocese, vicariate or prefecture apostolic.[8] A diocesan domicile would be had, for example, in the case of one who intended to reside forever within the boundaries of a certain diocese, without, however, intending to reside in any particular parish of that diocese.[9]

§3. *Terminology*

Canon 91

Persona dictur: *incola,* in loco ubi domicilium, *advena,* in loco ubi quasi-domocilium habet; *peregrinus,* si

[5] Canon 92, §§ 1, 2.

[6] Canon 93.

[7] Canon 92, § 3; cf. canon 216, § 3.

[8] Canon 92, §3.

[9] Vidal, *Jus Canonicum,* II, n. 11; Maroto, *Institutiones,* I, n. 410; *Epitome,* I, n. 183, "Potest igitur quispiam esse vagus in paroecia, et domicilium habere in diocesi."

versetur extra domicilium et quasi-domicilium quod adhuc retinet, *vagus*, si nullibi domicilium habeat vel quasi-domicilium.

The above regulation constitutes the canonical designation of persons, according as they possess a domicile or a quasi-domicile, or are without a domicile or a quasi-domicile, or are in a place outside of their domicile or quasi-domicile, which they still possess. In the present discussion it has been deemed best to retain the Latin terminology. The Latin terms have been canonized, as it were, by centuries of use, and their technical meaning is best preserved in the Latin language. English equivalents, it is feared, might beget confusion.

Incola. A person is called an *incola* in the place in which he has a domicile. This word has been employed in its present signification from the very beginning of the existence of the domicile as a legal institution. It was introduced by the Roman jurists,[10] accepted from the very beginning by the canonists,[11] and has been formally acknowledged by the Code.

Advena. A person is called an *advena* in the place where he has a quasi-domicile. As the quasi-domicile was unknown in Roman law, it is clear that the word advena in its present signification was used first by the canonists. At precisely what time it came to designate the possessor of a quasi-domicile is not clear. Sanchez[12] does not use the word. Laymann[13] and Pirhing[14] de-

[10] D. L., 16, 239, 2. "Incola est, qui aliqua regione domicilium suum contulit."

[11] Cf. Hostiensis in c. 10, *de sepult;* in c. 9, *de foro comp.*

[12] *De Matrimonio,* III, 18, n. 9 ff.

[13] *Theologia Moralis,* lib. V, tr. VI, c. 10, n. 6.

[14] Lib. II, tit. II, n. 18.

scribe the possessor of a quasi-domicile as a *quasi-incola,* while Benedict XIV[15] uses the expression *incola.* It is certain, however, that the term *advena* was in general use before the Code,[16] and the Code has not changed matters.

Peregrinus. A person is called a *peregrinus* when he is outside his domicile or quasi-domicile which he still retains. In Roman law the term itself *peregrinus* had a different meaning. It signified, in general, any free man who was not a Roman citizen.[17] At the same time, however, the idea of peregrinuty, as we understand it, is clearly implied in the famous definition of the Emperors,[18] wherein it is declared that, when a person is absent from his domicile to which he shall return, *"peregrinari videtur."* The word *peregrinus* has always been used in Canon law in its present meaning. It is retained by the Code.

Vagus. A *vagus* is a person who has neither a domicile or quasi-domicile in any place. The term *vagus,* in the technical sense it now bears, was not used in Roman law. Among the early canonists[19] the term vagabundus was more commonly used. Since the time of Sanchez, the present term (*vagus*) has been generally accepted.[20]

---

[15] Const. *"Inter Praeteritos,"* 3 Dec. 1749, n. 71 — *Fontes,* n. 404.

[16] D'Annibale, *Summula,* I, n. 85; Alberti, *De domicilio ecclesiastico,* n. 6; D'Angelo, *Il domicilio ecclesiastico.*

[17] Donnellus, *Com. in jure civ.* tit. 24, lib. VI, C. de Heredibus, l. 1.

[18] C. X., 40 (39), 7.

[19] Durandus, *Speculum Juris,* Lib. 1, pt. II, n. 30; Panormitanus, c. licet, *de foro comp.* n. 13.

[20] Sanchez, *De Matrimonio,* III, 25, n. 2; D'Annibale, *Summula,* I, n. 84.

CHAPTER VI

ACQUISITION OF DOMICILE AND QUASI-DOMICILE

Article I.—Acquisition of Domicile

Canon 92, §1. Domicilium acquiritur commoratione in aliqua paroecia aut quasi-paroecia, aut saltem in diocasi, vicariatu apostolico, praefectura apostolica; quae commoratio vel conjuncta sit cum animo ibi perpetuo manendi, vel sit protracta ad decennium completum.

The above regulation, while renewing for the most part the old legislation, contains the greatest innovation wrought by the new law in connection with domicile. Before the Code there was but one way of acquiring a domicile, viz., by actual residence in a place with the intention of remaining there permanently.[1] As a result of the new legislation there are now two distinct ways of acquiring a domicile:

(1) by residence in a place with the intention of remaining permanently, if nothing unforeseen should call one away.

(2) by residence alone continued for ten complete years.

---

[1] Sanchez, *De Matrimonio,* III, 23 n. 1-2; D'Annibale, *Summula,* I, § 83.

§1. *Acquisition of Domicile by Residence and Intention*

No change has been effected by the Code, in regard to this ancient and time honored method of acquiring a domicile. Both elements, habitation and intention, are required. Neither will suffice. A domicile constituted by this method is acquired at the very instant a person begins to reside in a place with the intention of remaining there permanently.[2]

A. *Residence*. As in the preceding legislation, this element consists in actual habitation in a place—personal physical presence in a place *per modum inhabitantis*.[3]

The residence must be personal. It is not enough that one buy or possess a home in a certain place; neither is it enough that one transfer the greater part of his belongings to a place. Merely material occupation of this character does not suffice. The theory of the sufficiency of mere material occupancy of a place, independently of personal presence, was advocated by the French canonist, Deshayes,[4] towards the close of the last century. Before the Code, this view was not accepted by even a single authority. In fact, it was opposed to the certain and unanimous teaching of canonists,[5] who, though admitting the usefulness of

[2] D'Annibale, op. cit., I, § 83; Vidal, *Jus Canonicum,* II, n. 11; *Epitome,* I, n. 183; Chelodi, *Jus de Personis,* n. 92; Farren, *Domicile and Quasi-Domicile,* p. 73.

[3] Schmalzgrueber, lib. II, tit. II, n. 9; Alberti, *De domicilio ecclesiastico,* n. 5; *Epitome,* I, n. 183; Vidal, op. cit., n. 11; Blat, *Commentarium,* n. 11; Toso, *Commentaria,* II, p. 19.

[4] *Questions Practiques sur le Mariage,* q. 6.

[5] *D'Annibale, Summula,* I, § 83, nota 11; Wernz, *Jus Decretalium,* IV, n. 177; Alberti, *De domicilio ecclesiastico,* n. 5; D'Angelo, *Il domicilio ecclesiastico,* p. 22.

material occupation as a proof of intention, never regarded it as constitutive of a domicile without personal presence. The view of Deshayes is clearly untenable under the New Code. The word *commoratio* etymologically and legally connotes a personal physical presence.[6] No other interpretation is admissible. No other is acknowledged by present day commentators.[7] The buying or renting of a house and the transferring of one's belongings are not only insufficient to constitute the residence required for the acquisition of a domicile; they are even entirely unnecessary.[8] The mere fact of personal residence is sufficient. A person may reside in a hotel or even in a furnished apartment, with practically little belonging to him. If he has the requisite intention, there is not the slightest doubt but that he has a domicile.[9]

The residence must be *per modum inhabitantis*. The exact signification of this characteristic of the residence is perhaps best seen in the light of some recent replies issuing from the various Congregations of the Roman Curia. In 1875, the Archbishop of Paris wrote

---

[6] Cf. Canon 1562, § 2; Canon 1720, § 1; Canons 2301, 2302.

[7] *Epitome*, I, n. 183; Blat, *Commentarium*, II, n. 11; D'Angelo, *Il domicilio ecclesiastico*, p. 22; Muniz, *Derecho Parroquial*, n. 77; Maroto, *Institutiones*, I, n. 411; Vidal, *Jus Canonicum*, II, n. 11.

[8] Schmalzgrueber, lib. II, tit. II, n. 9; D'Angelo, *Il domicilio ecclesiastico*, p. 22; D'Annibale, *Summula*, I, § 83; nota 11; Chelodi, *Jus de Personis*, n. 92; Maroto, *Institutiones*, I, n. 411, nota 3, "In jure canonico necessarium non est ad acquirendum domicilium ut domus ematur vel conducatur, aut bona ibi transferantur; sufficit quoad factum, RESIDENTIA."

[9] S. R. Rota *in Causa Gratianopolitana*, 8 April 1913 in Decisiones Coram Lega, dec. XXXVI, n. 10, "Duo ad domicilium requiruntur, viz., factum habitationis personalis et animus ibi commorandi." Maroto, *l. c.;* Blat, *Commentarium*, II, n. 11; Chelodi, *Jus de Personis*, n. 92.

to the Congregation of the Inquisition, declaring that it was not unusual in his diocese "that a person who desired to marry seemed to have a twofold domicile: the one, public, known, fixed, permanent, where he carried on his business, commercial and industrial affairs; the other, equally public, fixed and permanent where he slept, lived with his family, where he entertained his friends, and where all the affairs of family life were conducted." This state of affairs was not without difficulties, and hence the Archbishop of Paris requested the Sacred Congregation to determine whether there was but one true domicile, or whether the person in the case had a twofold domicile. The Sacred Congregation, on the 12 of May 1875, answered that the true domicile was that in which the person slept and lived with his family.[10] This principle was adopted by the Sacred Congregation of the Council, on the 18 of August 1906, in a Paris case involving the nullity of a marriage. A certain person had alleged the possession of two domiciles: one in which he resided and slept; the other in which he spent the hours of the day, conducting his business affairs. The Sacred Congregation admitted the first domicile but rejected the latter.[11] In another marriage case, this very same teaching was accepted and defended by the officials of the Sacred Roman Rota. They decided that that domicile only is recognized as such in which the night is spent.[12]

---

[10] S. C. Inq. 12 May, 1875—*Le Canoniste Contemporain*, vol. 33 (1910), 371.

[11] S.C.C. *in Causa Parisien*, 18 Aug. 1906—*Thesaurus Resol. S.C.C.* vol. 165, pp. 1027-1044. "Idea larium maxime verificatur de domo *in qua* dormiunt."

[12] S. R. Rota *in Causa Parisien*, 24 March 1911,—*A.A.S.*, III

It would seem then that to dwell in a place after the manner of an inhabitant, it is not enough to spend the hours of the day there. One must live there, spend the night there, have there his hearthstone (*lares*), however meagre and barren that may be.[13] In this connection, it must be remembered that it is not necessary, in order to acquire a domicile, that the residence extend over any determined length of time. Canonists have always taught that at the very moment one begins to dwell in a place with the intention of remaining, a domicile is acquired.[14] The new law has introduced no change.[15]

Finally, it is not necessary that the residence be physically continuous. A morally continuous residence is sufficient. A person, therefore, may leave his place of domicile for a vacation, a business trip, for any reason whatsoever, no matter how long he may be absent, provided he has the intention of returning.[16]

B. *Intention.* No change has been effected in this element by the Code. In addition, therefore, to the

---

(1911), p. 324 ff. "Sed iterum dico, multo magis collocatus est in loco ubi lares habent . . . ibi dormiendo etc. . . . quam in loco ubi negatiationi tantum aut labori vocat, quia secundum communem hominum aestimationem, praecipuum elementum collocationis ad domicilum requisitae est larium constitutio."

[13] De Smet, *De Sponsalibus et Matrimonio,* n. 45; Cappello, *De Matrimonio,* n. 682.

[14] Sanchez, *De Matrimonio,* III, 23, 2; Engel, lib. II, tit. II, n. 7; D'Annibale, *Summula,* I, § 83.

[15] Vidal, *Jus Canonicum,* II, n. 11; *Epitome,* I, n. 183; Chelodi, *Jus de Personis,* n. 92; De Meester, *Compendium,* I, n. 316; Maroto, *Institutiones,* I, n. 411.

[16] Canon. 95. Cf. Schmalzgrueber, lib. II, tit. II, n. 9; Vidal, *Jus Canonicum,* II, n. 11; De Meester, *Compendium,* I, n. 316; Toso, *Commentaria,* II, p. 19; Coronata, *Institutiones,* I, n. 124; Santamaria, *Comentarios al Codigo Canonico,* vol. I, p. 127.

actual personal residence in a place, one must have the intention of remaining there permanently, if nothing unforeseen occurs. This intention of permanent residence excludes neither the intention of temporary departures nor a future change of domicile. It implies merely that the intention of mere transitory residence must not at present exist.

In the first place the intention of permanent residence is not vitiated or affected by the fact that one has the intention of departing at stated and even frequent intervals, e.g., by reason of business or for a vacation, since it is not necessary that the residence be physically continuous. The Roman law made express provision for temporary departures of this kind when it declared that under these circumstances "when a person has left the place he is considered to be a wanderer, and when he has returned, he is regarded as having given up his wandering state."[17] Pre-Code authorities have always recognized this as an established principle.[18] The Code has not changed matters, and commentators on the new law have fully accepted this teaching.[19]

Secondly, this intention need not be absolute and irrevocable, as if one must renounce all right to change his domicile and resolve to remain in the present domicile always, no matter what may happen—under every possible circumstance. An intention so fixed and im-

[17] C. X. 40 (39) 7; H. Dernberg, *System des Römischen Rechts*, n. 38; Savigny, *System des Heutigen Römischen Rechts*, VIII, 353.

[18] Schmalzgrueber, lib. II, tit. II, n. 9; Lega, *De Judiciis*, I, n. 337; Alberti, *De domicilio ecclesiastico*, n. 5; D'Angelo, *Il domicilio ecclesiastico*, p. 23 ff.

[19] Vidal, *Jus Canonicum*, II, n. 11; *Epitome*, I, n. 183; Toso, *Commentaria*, II, p. 19; De Meester, *Compendium*, I, n. 316.

mutable was required neither by the Roman law, nor by the ancient canon law. On the contrary, the possibility of a future change was considered quite compatible with the intention required to constitute a domicile. In fact, this is plainly implied in the clause "*si nihil inde avocet*" contained in the famous definition of the Emperors,[20] which was received without change into canon law.[21] The clause "*si nihil inde avocet*" has always been interpreted as indicating that an intention of indefinite stability (*perpetuitas proposita*) is clearly sufficient, i.e., in order to have the requisite intention, it is sufficient that one here and now intend to remain in a place permanently, unless something, at present unforeseen, may cause him to change his mind. If nothing untoward happens, one will remain here; if unforeseen circumstances arise, he will change his present determination, and hence, his domicile.[22] The words "*si nihil inde avocet,*" then, are entirely opposed to an irrevocable and efficacious permanent intention, and clearly imply that the intention may subsequently be revoked on account of some supervening cause. This doctrine is completely in harmony with human experience. It is the exception, not the rule, that a man will positively and definitely intend to remain in a place *usque ad supremum diem*. No one knows what

[20] C. X. 40 (39) 7.

[21] S. R. Rota *in Causa Gratianopolitana*, 8 April 1913, in *Decisiones Coram Lega*, dec. XXXVI, n. 5, "notio canonica domicilii continetur expresse in C. X. 40 (39) 7.

[22] Sanchez, *In Decal.*, lib. IV, c. 39, n. 20; Engel, lib. I, tit. XI, n. 27; Pichler, *Epitome juris canonici*, lib. II, tit. II, n. 24; La Croix, *Theologia Moralis*, lib. IV, p. 2, n. 2184; Alberti, *De domicilio ecclesiastico*, n. 5; Chelodi, *Jus de Personis*, n. 92; De Meester, *Compendium*, I, n. 316; Vlaming, *Praelectiones juris matrimonii*, I, n. 65.

the future holds in store for him. A person's outlook on life may become so different, or circumstances may so alter his social or economic position, as to cause him to completely change the old order of things. As one writer aptly remarks, "An immutable resolution is unreasonable in itself, untrue to life, and not required by human legislation."[23]

In this connection, two points are to be particularly noted. In the first place, if a person prudently forsees that he will, at some future date, depart for some reason, his intention will remain suspended and inefficacious.[24] Secondly, if a person is certain that at some future date he will change his residence, it is clear that he has not the intention of permanent residence. The idea of permanence clearly excludes any present intention of transitory residence. Therefore, if a person, for example, accepts a position which he knows will last for a period of twelve years, and intends to reside in the place for that period of time, he will not have the intention of permanent residence, and therefore he will not acquire a domicile by this first method of acquisition.[25]

Expert canonical opinion has always regarded the clause *"si nihil inde avocet"* as representing a resolutive condition, which does not change one's present will, and does not prevent one from having the intention necessary to constitute a domicile.[26] On the other

[23] O'Donnell, Domicile,—*Irish Theological Quarterly,* XI (1916), 304.

[24] La Croix, *Theologia Moralis,* lib. IV, p. 2, n. 2184; O'Donnell, *l. c.*

[25] Such a person will have a domicile at the expiration of ten years. Canon 92, 1.

[26] D'Annibale, *Summula,* I, § 83, nota 12. "Sed 'si nihil avocet' conditio resolutiva est quae praesentem voluntatem non mutat"; Alberti, *De domicilio ecclesiastico,* n. 5; D'Angelo, *Il domicilio*

hand, authorities are agreed that a suspensive condition does affect one's present will; it suspends it and prevents one from having the requisite intention.[27]

A few definitions here may serve to simplify matters. A condition has been defined by theologians as a circumstance or quality attached to an act, on the existence of which the act depends.[28] The condition has been divided into a resolutive condition and a suspensive condition. A resolutive condition is one which, when fulfilled, puts an end to an act already placed. An example would be: "I give you this home, but if I should become penniless, it must be returned to me." A suspensive condition is one, on the fulfillment of which the action depends. An example would be: "I will go to Canada, if you give me your car."[29] Applying these principles to domiciliary intention, two cases may be considered. In the first case, a person intends to remain in a place permanently unless something unforeseen should cause him to revoke his intention and establish himself elsewhere. Authorities declare that such a condition does not affect or change one's present intention, since the intention does not depend on any particular condition known at the present

---

ecclesiastico, p. 23, nota 1; Chelodi, *Jus de Personis,* n. 92; De Meester, *Compendium,* I, n. 316. This is clear also from the fact that all canonists embody this clause in their definition of domicile.

[27] D'Annibale, *l. c.* "Nam conditio suspensiva voluntatem suspendit"; Alberti, *l. c.;* D'Angelo, l. c., *Epitome,* I, n. 183; Maroto, *Institutiones,* I, n. 411, nota 3. "Voluntas manendi in aliquo loco non sufficiebat ad domicilium acquirendum si subjiciebatur *condicioni suspensivae.*" S. R. Rota in Causa Parisien, 5 May 1914 in A.A.S., VI (1914), 397.

[28] D'Annibale, *Summula,* I, § 41; Aertnys-Damen, *Theologia Moralis,* I, n. 861.

[29] Cf. D'Annibale, *l. c.;* Aertnys-Damen, *l. c.*

time.[30] This condition merely indicates that the intention may subsequently be revoked because of some unforeseen ensuing cause. On the fulfillment of the condition, one changes his intention (which was entirely sufficient) and the domicile secured on the strength of that intention ceases to exist.

In the second case, one intends to remain in a place permanently, if, for example, he can secure in this place a satisfactory position. All authorities are agreed that such an intention is ineffective and insufficient to acquire a domicile.[31] In this case, no one can say that a person has the intention of permanently residing in a place if his intention *from the very beginning* is known to be subject to certain conditions, and if he might cease at any moment to remain in the place on account of the non-fulfillment of these conditions. Until the condition is fulfilled the intention remains suspended, and therefore a domicile is not contracted. This doctrine was confirmed by a recent decision of the Roman Rota,[32] in which it was declared that the taking up of residence with the intention to remain if marriage followed, was not sufficient to establish a domicile.

§2. *Acquisition of Domicile by Residence alone*

The second method of acquiring a domicile, according to the New Code, is by sole actual residence in a

[30] D'Annibale, *Summula,* I, § 83, nota 12; D'Angelo, *Il domicilio ecclesiastico,* p. 23, note 1; Alberti, *De domicilio ecclesiastico,* n. 5; De Meester, *Compendium,* I, n. 316; Chelodi, *Jus de Personis,* n. 92; Muniz, *Derecho Parroquial,* n. 78; Toso, *Commentaria,* II, p. 19.

[31] D'Annibale, *l. c.,* Maroto, *Institutiones,* I, n. 411, nota 3; Toso, *l. c.;* Muniz, *l. c.; Epitome,* I, n. 183.

[32] S. R. Rota *in Causa Parisien,* 5 May 1914, in *A.A.S.,* VI (1914), p. 397.

place for a period of ten complete years.[33] This regulation constitutes the greatest innovation introduced by the New Code.

The ten years residence has had an interesting history in connection with the development of the domicile. In Roman law, as a result of a decree of the Emperor Hadrian,[34] it constituted a presumption as to the existence of a domicile in the case of students. In the great Glossa on the Corpus Juris Civilis, composed by the jurists of Bologna, this presumption was extended to every class of persons.[35] The early canonists[36] accepted this presumption with its universal application, and it remained until the publication of the Code as one of the principal indications (adminicula) that a person had established a domicile.[37] The ten years residence has reached its final development in the Code, wherein it is declared that such residence is sufficient of itself to constitute a domicile.[38]

It may be mentioned here that some authors[39] do not speak correctly when they declare that a residence of ten years constitutes a *praesumptio juris et de jure* in favor of a domicile. According to the new law a residence of ten years is constitutive of a domicile; it

---

[33] Canon 92, § 1.

[34] C. X. 40 (39) 2.

[35] Gloss on C. X. 40 (39) 2.

[36] Hostiensis in c. 20, *de decimis;* Panormitanus, in c. 14, *de foro comp.* n. 4.

[37] Sanchez, *de Matrimonio,* III, 23, 2; Schmalzgrueber, lib. II, tit. II, n. 12; Lega, *De Judiciis,* I, n. 337; D'Annibale, *Summula,* I, § 83, nota 13. S. R. Rota *in Causa Ravennaten,* 15 May 1911—*A.A.S.,* III (1911), p. 488.

[38] Canon 92, § 1.

[39] De Meester, *Compendium, I,* n. 316; De Smet, *De Spons. et Matr.* n. 45.

really gives one a domicile. This is clear from the disjunctive proposition enunciated in Canon 92, §1: A domicile is *acquired* in two ways, either by residence with the intention of remaining or by residence for ten complete years.[40]

Unlike the domicile constituted by residence and intention, which is acquired as soon as both elements are simultaneously present, the domicile constituted by sole residence is not acquired until the expiration of ten complete years.[41]

It is abundantly clear from Canon 92, §1, that in acquiring a domicile by this second method there is no need of an intention of remaining. Indeed, the fact that one had a contrary intention would not prevent him from acquiring a domicile, provided he resided in the place for the time required by the law.[42] All that is required by the law is that a person reside in a place for ten complete years, no matter what his intention may be. By that token a domicile is acquired.[43]

What has been said of the residence in the first

---

[40] Vidal, *Jus Canonicum,* II, n. 11; Bouuaert-Simenon, *Manuale juris canonici,* n. 242, § 3; Coronata, *Institutiones,* I, n. 124, nota 3; Chelodi, *Jus de Personis,* n. 92. "Si habitatio jam ad decennium completum protracta fuerit, *verum inducit domicilium,* non amplius meram praesumptionem juris et de jure."

[41] De Meester, *Compendium,* I, n. 316, "Per commorationem ad decennium protractam domicilium acquiritur a *completo* termino commorationis." Bouuaert-Simenon, op. cit., n. 242; *Epitome,* I, n. 183.

[42] Vidal, *Jus Canonicum,* II, n. 11; Muniz, *Derecho Parroquial,* I, n. 78; Bouuaert-Simenon.

[43] De Meester, *Compendium,* I, n. 316, "Hodierno jure . . . domicilium contrabitur per solam commorationem protractam ad decennium completum, quidquid sit de intentione manendi, dummodo constet de commoratione materiale." Bouuaert-Simenon, *l. c.*. Vidal, *l. c.;* Muniz, *l. c.*

method of acquiring a domicile applies also to this residence.[44] Therefore actual personal residence *per modum inhabitantis* is required. The residence required here differs from the residence described above only in its duration. It is this aspect alone, therefore, which requires consideration.

The law declares that the residence must be prolonged to ten complete years. This ten year period is to be computed according to Canon 34, §3, 1° and 3°.[45] The months and years, therefore, are to be taken as they are in the calendar.[46] Since, as a general rule, the starting point does not coincide with the beginning of the day, the first day, being incomplete, is not counted, and the time ends with the last day of the same number.[47] Supposing then that the ten years' residence begins on the 20th day of June, 1920, it is completed with the end of the 20th day of June, 1930, or the beginning of the 21st day of June, 1930.[48]

Although the Code declares merely that the ten years' residence must be complete, it is quite clear that this period must also be a continuous one. The words themselves, "*protracta ad decennium,*" clearly indicate the notion of continuity, and this indication is confirmed by the unanimous teaching of canonists,[49] and

---

[44] Vidal, *Jus Canonicum,* II, n. 11.

[45] De Meester, *Compendium,* I, n. 316; nota 6; Muniz, *Derecho Parroquial,* I, n. 78; Blat, *Commentarium,* II, n. 11; Cocchi, *Commentarium,* II, n. 21.

[46] Canon 34, § 3, 1°.

[47] Canon 34, § 3, 3°.

[48] Canon 34, § 3, 3°; Muniz, *Derecho Parroquial,* t. 1, n. 78; De Meester, *Compendium,* I, n. 316, nota 6.

[49] Vidal, *Jus Canonicum,* II, n. 11; De Meester, op. cit., n. 316; Bouuaert-Simenon, *Manuale juris canonici,* n. 242; Ayrinhac, *General Legislation,* n. 196; *Muniz, l. c.,* Blat, *Commentarium,* II, n. 11.

by an analogy with the month's residence of the decree *"Ne Temere,"* which was interpreted by canonists generally as implying a continuous month.[50] It is to be noted, however, that a physical continuity is not required; a morally continuous residence suffices.[51]

The question naturally arises—a question not without some difficulty—in what way is this continuity broken? The Code gives no indication and, since no other official declaration has been given, a solution must be sought by appealing to Canon 20. According to this canon when there is lacking an express prescription of law on some point, a norm is to be taken from laws given in similar cases; from the general principles of law applied with canonical equity; from the practice of the Roman Curia; and from the common and constant teaching of canonists. But two of these will be of service, viz., the similar law—the month's residence—and the teaching of canonists regarding the month's residence and the ten years' residence.

In general, two things have been regarded as affecting the continuity of the residence, viz., an absence of a certain length, and any absence, however brief, accompanied by an intention of not returning. Each of these shall be considered.

Absence alone: In connection with the month's residence, according to the common interpretation, an absence of one or another day would not affect the

---

[50] Wernz, *Jus Decretalium,* IV, n. 188, p. 294; Wouters, *De Forma Promissionis et Celebrationis Matrimonii,* n. 33; Rossi, *De Celebratione Matrimonii,* n. 56, nota 77; Cappello, *De Matrimonio,* n. 685; Vermeersch, *De forma Spons. et Matr.,* n. 58.

[51] Vidal, *l. c.;* De Meester, *l. c.;* Bouuaert-Simenon, *l. c.;* Ayrinhac, *l. c.*

continuity.[52] It would appear from this that an absence of more than just a few days, e.g., four or five days, would interrupt the continuity.[53] Applying this rule, *servatis servandis,* to the ten years' residence, it would seem that a continuous absence of one year would break the continuity, while an absence of three or four months would not. Coming to the teaching of present day commentators in regard to the ten years' residence, one does not find a complete harmony of opinion. Some canonists[54] incline to the view that a continuous absence of more than six months will break the continuity of the residence. Cappello[55] declares that a residence of five or six months each year for ten years will be sufficient to constitute a domicile. Vermeersch[56] is even more liberal. According to him, a residence of about four months each year for the ten year period will be enough to acquire a domicile. From the combined opinion of the foregoing authorities the following norm may be established. It appears quite certain that continuous absence for a year would break the continuity of the residence. It would seem more probable that a continuous absence of over six months would have the same effect. In view of the authority Vermeersch enjoys, and in view also of the fact that a man can have at least three domiciles[57] by residing

---

[52] Wernz, *l. c.;*Wouters, *l. c.;* Vermeersch, *l. c.;* Noldin, *Decretum de Spons. et Matr.,* n. 10.

[53] Wernz, *l. c.*

[54] Bouuaert-Simenon, *Manuale juris canonici,* n. 242; Farren, *Domicile and Quasi-domicile,* p. 86; Kinane, "Domicile"—*Irish Ecclesiastical Record,* 5 Series, vol. 11, pp. 224-225.

[55] *De Matrimonio,* n. 683.

[56] *Epitome,* I, n. 183.

[57] Cf. page 154.

three or four months in each, it is difficult to deny probability to his opinion.

It is to be noted that the continuity of the residence is broken by a sufficiently long absence, even though one has the intention of returning. Intention has no part in this second method of acquiring a domicile.

Absence with the intention of not returning: Does any absence with the intention of not returning break the continuity of the residence? This question arose shortly after the decree *"Ne Temere"* in connection with the month's residence. A sharp controversy ensued, but according to the common and more probable opinion departure from a place with the intention of not returning did not affect the continuity, if, of course, the departure did not last more than a day or two.[58] The month's residence, according to these canonists, was to be computed independently of intention. The material fact of residence alone was to be considered. The month's residence had been introduced precisely to do away with the difficulties attendant upon the element of intention; if this element were to be required the very end of the law would be defeated.

Can the same line of reasoning be validly applied to the ten years' residence? Farren,[59] who discusses this question at some length, answers in the negative. According to him, the continuity of the residence is broken by any absence, no matter how brief, if it is accompanied by the intention of not returning.[60] Far-

[58] Wernz, *Jus Decretalium,* IV, n. 188; Wouters, *o. c.,* p. 33; Gennari, *Il Monitore Ecclesiastico,* Series II, vol. X, p. 90; Noldin, *o. c.,* n. 10; Cappello, *o. c.,* n. 685; Damen, *Theologia Moralis,* II, n. 840.

[59] *Domicile and Quasi-domicile,* pp. 80 ff.

[60] Farren, *o. c.,* p. 85.

ren, first of all, denies the parity between a domicile secured by residence and the month's residence. "Canon 95," he declares, "states that a domicile is lost by departure with the intention of not returning. This is a general statement, and applies even to the domicile secured by the ten years' residence, so that unlike the month's residence, this domicile is lost by any absence with the intention of not returning. The result is there is not a complete parity between the month's residence and the domicile secured by ten years' residence. Consequently, we cannot say that, since intention plays no part in determining the continuity of the residence in the one case, neither does it affect the continuity in the other."[61] Farren then offers the following argument: Whatever interrupts the continuity of the residence after the completion of the ten years' period will interrupt the continuity of the residence before the completion of that period. But absence even for a short time with the intention of not returning interrupts the residence after the ten-year period (as otherwise the domicile would not be lost). Therefore, absence even for a short time with the intention of not returning interrupts the residence before the completion of the ten years' period."[62] This opinion is also defended by Kinane, and, it would seem, by Vermeersch[63] and Cappello.[64]

It cannot be admitted that this opinion enjoys that

---

[61] Farren, *o. c.*, pp. 83-84.

[62] Farren, *o. c.*, p. 84.

[63] Vermeersch, *Epitome,* I, n. 183, "Quocirca, si quis per decem annos locum quempiam stabiliter per quatuor menses, singulis annis, inhabitaverit, nec umquam animo linquendi locum discess erit . . . habebit domicilium in illo loco."

[64] *De Matrimonio,* n. 683—Cappello's statement, with the exception of the time, is the same as that of Vermeersch.

certainty which would label it the only true opinion on this matter, for the reason that the arguments advanced in its favor do not appear to be conclusive.

It is declared that there is no parity between the domicile secured by residence and the month's residence. This is entirely true, but it is not the question. The question is concerning the parity between *the residence which secures a domicile* and the month's residence, not between the *domicile already secured by residence* and the month's residence. The writer clearly confuses the domicile secured by residence with the residence itself. His argument, therefore, proves nothing.

The syllogistic argument which Farren offers takes for granted a very fundamental point which, it would seem, is unjustified. He sees a complete parity between a domicile already secured and the residence by which it is secured. This parity is denied. The domicile is a juridical entity; the residence, on the other hand, is a mere material fact which under certain conditions gives rise to the domicile. The residence is the cause; the domicile is the effect. The two are entirely distinct. Again, it is certain from Canon 95 that a domicile is not lost by any absence, however great, provided one has the intention of returning. On the other hand, all authorities agree that the ten years' residence is broken by an absence of one year, even though one has the intention of returning. Since the parity between a domicile and the residence which secures it is not true, the argument which is based on it falls.

It cannot be thought, then, that that opinion is the true one, which declares that any absence, however brief, if accompanied by an intention of not returning, destroys the continuity.

Can anything be said in favor of the opinion which declares that a brief departure with the intention of not returning does not break the continuity? Two considerations may be advanced in support of this opinion: the words and end of the law, and the interpretation of canonists in regard to the month's residence. (1) The history of domicile and quasi-domicile have manifested the great difficulties attendant upon the intentional element. Indeed, these difficulties were so acute and, at times, so seemingly incapable of solution that many eminent authorities expressed the desire that the ecclesiastical authorities change or modify the law.[65] In answer to the plea to remove these difficulties, the legislator has introduced a new method of acquiring a domicile, in which only one condition is prescribed, viz., residence for ten complete years. In estimating the ten years, then, objective facts alone should be considered. The whole quesiton of intention must be completely disregarded; otherwise the very end of the law will be defeated. If, therefore, a person resides in a place for a sufficient length of time each year for ten complete years, he must be regarded as being an inhabitant of that place—as having acquired a domicile there, no matter what his intention may be. To say that any more is required is to violate the end of the law and the words of the legislator. (2) Again, in regard to the month's residence, many canon-

[65] Gasparri, *De Matrimonio*, n. 1089; Langonio, Votum—*Anal. Eccl.*, vol. XIII (1905), p. 451 ff. "Dico . . . fieri potest necessaria modificatio, videlicet (1): statuendo, quod propter *solum factum* commorationis, ad tale taleve tempus . . . acquiratur quasi-domicilium canonicum."

ists[66] declared that even if a person departed (for a day or two) with the intention of not returning, his residence was not interrupted. There seems to be no reason why this teaching cannot be applied to the ten years' residence. The parity between the month's residence and the ten years' residence, it may be admitted, is incomplete, but only in the sense that they differ in relation to time and in regard to effect, i.e., the one merely gives a pastor competence to lawfully assist at a marriage,[67] the other is capable of constituting a domicile.[68] That the parity is not complete in regard to the continuity is not proved. As in the month's residence, so also in the ten years' residence, one condition only is required, *solum factum commorationis.* When that condition is fulfilled a domicile is acquired. In our opinion, the burden of proof rests on those who, in the face of the clear wording of the Code, would demand any more.

The great difficulty connected with this opinion is that, with one probable exception, it has not the support of extrinsic authority. The probable exception is Roberti. We say probable because it is only indirectly and implicity, though really, we think, that he seems to favor this opinion. He says, *"Post decem annos completos acquiritur domicilium . . . independenter a quocumque interno elemento."*[69]

In conclusion, great probability, especially in view of

---

[66] Gennarri,—*Monitore Ecclesiastico,* Series 2, Vox. X, p. 90; Wernz, *Jus Decretalium,* IV, n. 188; Noldin, *Decretum de Spons. et Matr.,* n. 10; Wouters, *l. c.;* Cappello, *De Matrimonio,* n. 685; Damen, *Theologia Moralis,* II, n. 840.

[67] Canon 1097, § 1, 2°.

[68] Canon 92, § 1.

[69] Roberti, *De Processibus,* I, n. 63, p. 118.

the authorities defending it, cannot be denied to the opinion which declares that a brief departure with the intention of not returning destroys the continuity of the residence. It would seem, however, that the opposite view is not without some probability.

Article II.—Acquisition of Quasi-Domicile

Canon 92, §2. Quasi-domicilium acquiritur commoratione uti supra, quae vel coniuncta sit cum ibi manendi saltem ad maiorem anni partem, si nihil inde avocet, vel sit reapse protracta ad maiorem anni partem.

Before the Code there was but one way of acquiring a quasi-domicile, namely, by actual residence in a place with the intention of remaining there for the greater part of a year.[70] As in the case of domicile, a new method has been added by the Code, viz., actual residence for the greater part of a year. In the new legislation, therefore, there are two ways of securing a quasi-domicile: (1) by actual residence with the intention of remaining for the greater part of a year, if nothing unforseen occurs; (2) by actual residence prolonged for the greater part of the year.

§1. *Acquisition of Quasi-Domicile by Residence and Intention.*

No change has been introduced by the New Code in regard to this method of acquiring a quasi-domicile. The similarity between this method of acquiring a

[70] S. C. S. Off., litt. encycl., 7 June, 1867, "Ad constituendum quasi-domicilium . : . duo simul requiruntur: habitatio nempe in eo loco ubi matrimonium contrabitur, atque animus ibi permanendi per majorem anni partem." Cf. Gasparri, *De Matrimonio*, n. 916.

quasi-domicile and a domicile is obvious. As a matter of fact the similarity between the two—they differ only in relation to the element of time—has always been indicated by canonists.[71] What has been said, therefore, concerning the nature of the residence and intention in connection with the domicile is to be applied, servatis servandis, to the quasi-domicile. Two points only need explanation: the nature of the intention, and the precise signification of the phrase *"ad majorem anni partem"*.

Intention: It is important to note that in order to secure a quasi-domicile by this first method, the intention must cover the time in advance, i. e., it must exist from the very beginning of the period it influences. Subsequent ratification is not enough, and any period that elapsed before the intention was formed must be left out of consideration when the test is being applied as to whether or not a quasi-domicile has been acquired. A person, therefore, who, having resided in a place for four months, now intends to remain for three or four more months, has not the requisite intention, and therefore will not acquire a quasi-domicile until he has actually lived there for the greater part of the year. In a word, the intention must be such as to give to the whole period of the residence a moral unity.

Ad majorem anni partem: The Code, practically repeating the legislation of the Instruction of the

---

[71]Suarez, lib. II, *De diebus festis,* c. XIV, n. 6; Sanchez, *de Matrimonio,* III, 23, n. 14; Schmalzgrueber, lib. II, tit. NN, n. 17; D'Annibale, *Summula,* I, n. 84; Vidal, *Jus Canonicum,* II, n. 12; Chelodi, *Jus de Personis,* n. 92; "Quasi-domicilium est ad instar domicilii." Muniz, *Derecho Parroquial,* I, n. 82.

Holy Office of 1867[72] employs the phrase "*ad majorem anni partem*" to indicate the length of time required for the constitution of a quasi-domicile. As noted above some canonists[73] were very liberal in their interpretation as to what residence was sufficient to constitute a quasi-domicile. Lombardi[74] and Lehmkuhl[75] declared that a notable part of the year was sufficient, the latter considering four months as a notable part. Others[76] were content with a vague "some months". Before the Code, as mentioned above,[77] none of these opinions could be termed probable. The Code confirms—if confirmation were necessary—their improbability.[78]

The difficulty lies in determining what constitutes the greater part of the year. Some canonists[79] interpret the greater part of a year as being a period of at least six months. Other canonists[80] require a period of residence that extends beyond six months—*ultra semestre.*

---

[72] S. C. S. Off., litt. encycl., 7 June 1867—*Collect. S. C. P. F.*, n. 1303.

[73] Lombardi, *Inst. Juris Canonici Privati,* III, 187 Lehmkuhl, *Theol. Moral.*, II, n. 775.

[74] *L. c.*

[75] *L. c.*

[76] Ballerini Palmieri, *Opus Theologicum Morale,* VI, tr. 10, n. 1186.

[77] Cf. page 89 ff.

[78] Canon 92, § 1; Vidal, *Jus Canonicum,* II, n. 11; Chelodi, *Jus de Personis,* n. 92; *Epitome,* I, n. 184; Prummer, *Theologia Moralis,* I, n. 193.

[79] Maroto, *Institutiones,* I, n. 410; Blat, *Commentarium,* II, n. 11; Damen, *Theologia Moralis,* I, n. 149; Bouuaert-Simenon, *Manuale juris canonici,* n. 243; Vlaming, *Prael. juris matrimonii,* n. 66; Cocchi, *Commentarium,* II, p. 21.

[80] Vidal, *Jus Canonicum,* II, n. 11; *Epitome,* I, n. 184; Chelodi, *Jus de Personis,* n. 92; Prummer, *Theologia Moralis,* I, n. 193; De Meester, *Compendium,* I, n. 317.

Certainly, taking them in their ordinary signification, the words "for the greater part of a year" clearly indicate a period in excess of six months. Again, before the Code, the Roman authorities had no sympathy with the view that the greater part of the year could be interpreted as meaning six months. In a Paris case involving the validity of a marriage, decided by the Sacred Congregation of the Council on August 28, 1898 [81] it was expressly declared that the phrase *"ad majorem anni partem"* was to be interpreted as indicating a period beyond six months.[82] This teaching was confirmed by the officials of the Rota in two recent cases, wherein they rejected the opinion that an intention of residing six months was sufficient to constitute a quasi-domicile.[83] Since the Code this opinion has been defended by such eminent canonists as Vidal,[84] Vermeersch-Creusen,[85] Chelodi,[86] Cappello,[87] De Smet[88] and many others.[89]

---

[81] S. C. C. *in Causa Parisen,* 28 Aug. 1898—*A.S.S.* XXXI, p. 365.

[82] S. C. C. *in Causa Parisien,* 28 Aug. 1898—*A.S.S.* XXXI, p. 365. "Ad contrabendum quasi domicilium auctoritate S. Officii et S. C. C. requiritur factum commorationis cum intentione ibidem manendi per majorem anni partem, idest, ultra semestre."

[83] S. R. Rota *in Causa Ravennaten,* 29 Dec. 1911—*A.A.S.,* IV (1912), p. 327, "Nequit approbari sententia illorum, qui doceant ad quasi-domicilium acquirendum sufficere sex menses . . . Intentio quae ex sacris canonibus requiritur . . . est ea quae extendit ad majorem anni partem, non vero ad sex tantum menses." S. R. Rota *in Causa Parisien,* 24 April 1914—*A.A.S.,* VI (1914), pp. 409-410.

[84] *Jus Canonicum,* II, p. 11.

[85] *Epitome,* I, n. 184.

[86] *Jus de Personis,* n. 92.

[87] *De Matrimonio,* n. 680.

[88] *De Spons, et Matr.,* n. 47.

[89] De Meester, *Compendium,* I, n. 317; Badii, *Institutiones juris canonici,* p. 83; Prummer, *Theologia Moralis,* I, n. 193.

What may be said of the opinion interpreting the greater part of the year as indicating a period of six months? Vlaming[90] and Bouuaert-Simeon,[91] who defend this opinion, although admitting that strictly speaking the greater part of the year signifies a period of time slightly in excess of six months, nevertheless declare that it is sufficient to intend to reside for at least six months. These writers argue from the Holy Office Instruction of 1867, according to which by virtue of Canon 6, 3°. the present law is to be interpreted. In the Instruction it is declared that a conclusive proof of the intention of remaining the greater part of the year may be gleaned from the fact that a person has established himself in a place for six months (*ad sex menses*). It is also alleged that before the Code a residence of six months was commonly regarded as sufficient.[92]

These arguments, however, have little value. In the first place, the argument from the Instruction is not a valid one. Nowhere in the Instruction is it declared that an intention to reside for six months is sufficient to constitute a quasi-domicile. Residence for *six months* is merely declared to be a *proof of the intention of remaining the greater part of the year.*

The second argument may be seriously questioned. Any opinion which is opposed by such prominent canonists as Gasparri,[93] D'Annibale,[94] and Wernz,[95] and

[90] *Prael. juris matrimonii*, n. 66.

[91] *Manuale juris canonici*, n. 243.

[92] Bouuaert-Simenon, *op. cit.*, n. 243.

[93] *De Matrimonio*, n. 916.

[94] *Summula*, I, § 84.

[95] *Jus Decretalium*, IV, n. 177. Cf. also the Votum of Wernz—*Anal. Eccl.*, Vol. VII (1899), 68.

by a number of decisions emanating from the Congregations of the Roman Curia, can hardly be termed probable.[96]

Speculatively speaking, we think that the first opinion is the truer and most probable. In view of the authorities[97] supporting the second view, it would seem that it is at least extrinsically probable.

Practically, however, the two opinions will hardly differ. Granting that six months are sufficient, since the time at which the intention and residence simultaneously occur will hardly ever coincide with the beginning of the day, the first day will not be counted and hence the period will always be a little in excess of six months. For example, a person comes to a place at three o'clock in the afternoon of June 20, intending to stay for six months. According to Canon 34, § 3, 3°, the six months' period will not expire until midnight of the 20th of December. There will have elapsed, therefore, six months and a few hours—*ultra semestre*—the greater part of the year.

§2. *Acquisition of Quasi-Domicile by Residence Alone*

The second method of acquiring a quasi-domicile is by residence alone for the greater part of the year. This method of securing a quasi-domicile differs from the similar method of acquiring a domicile only in respect to the length of time required. In all other respects,

---

[96] S. C. C., *In Causa Parisien,* 14 Dec. 1889—*A.S.S.*, XXII, p. 487; S. C. C. *in Causa Parisien,* 28 Aug. 1898—*A.S.S.*, XXXI, p. 365; S. R. Rota *in Causa Ravennaten,* 29 Dec. 1911—*A.A.S.*, IV (1914), p. 327; S. R. Rota *in Causa Parisien,* 24 April 1914—*A.A.S.*, VI (1914), pp. 409-410.

[97] Cf. authorities in note 79.

what has been said of the residence required for the acquisition of the domicile in this connection is to be applied to the quasi-domicile. The residence, therefore, must be personal, morally continuous, and computed according to Canon 34, § 3, 1° and 3°.[98]

The only point to be considered is the length of the absence required to break the continuity. As in the case of the domicile, a probable norm must be drawn from the combined teaching of canonists on the question,[99] and from an analogy with the months residence.

Arguing from the common interpretation[100] in regard to the month's residence, it would appear that an absence of six weeks would certainly interrupt the continuity, while an absence of a few (two or three) weeks would not affect the continuity.[101] Coming to the canonists, some declare that an absence of a few weeks would not affect the continuity.[102] Other writers[103] incline to the view that continuous absence for one month would interrupt the continuity. As one writer declares: "If continuous residence for a month is regarded as a presumption of the will to remain for the greater part of the year, it is reasonable to suppose that absence for a month would be sufficiently grave

---

[98] De Meester, *Compendium,* I, n. 318; Muniz, *Derecho Parroquial,* I, n. 78 and 82; Cocchi, *Commentarium,* II, p. 21.

[99] Canon 20.

[100] Cf. page 128.

[101] Cf. Farren, *Domicile and Quasi-Domicile,* p. 90.

[102] De Meester, *Compendium,* I, n. 318, p. 215, nota 4; Bouuaert-Simenon, *Manuale juris canonici,* n. 243, page 131, nota 5. "Si deficit animus, conditio commorationis non destruitur per breves absentias aliquot dierum, imo paucarum hebdomadarum."

[103] Kinane, "Domicile in the New Code" I. E. R., 5 series, vol. XI, p. 228; Farren, *o. c.,* p. 91.

interruption to break the moral continuity."[104] One canonist, Coronata,[105] declares that contiuous absence for a month would not interrupt the continuity.

From the composite opinion of the foregoing authorities, it would seem more probable that an absence of one month would break the continuity of the residence. It would seem that the view of Coronata may be regarded as probable, in view of that fact that the acquisition of a quasi-domicile is a *quid favorabile,*[106] and according to the well-known principle of law: *"favores convenit ampliari".*[107]

It is quite generally agreed that week-end absence, even though repeated each week, as in the case of students and teachers, would not destroy the continuity.[108]

---

[104] Farren, *o. c.,* p. 91.

[105] *Institutiones,* I, n. 125.

[106] Cf. S. C. S. *in Causa Parisien,* 28 July 1906—*Thesaurus Resol. S.C.C.,* Vol. 165, p. 882 ff. "Reapse quod quis habet domicilium . . . multo magis debemus ampliare quam restringere, potissimum in jure nostro, in quo considerantur domicilium et quasi-domicilium in ordine ad sacra recipienda, seu ad exercenda jura et officia Christiana, quae omnia pertingunt ad media sanctificationis." Cf. also S. R. Rota *in Causa Gratianopolitant,* 8 April 1913—*Decisiones Coram Lega,* dec. XXXVI, n. 13.

[107] Reg. 15, R. J. in Sexto.

[108] De Meester, *Compendium,* I, n. 318, p. 215, note 4; Bouuaert-Simenon, *o. c.,* n. 243; Farren, *l. c.*

CHAPTER VII

LOSS OF DOMICILE AND QUASI-DOMICILE

Article I—Loss of Domicile

Canon 95—Domicilium et quasi-domicilium amittitur discessione a loco cum animo non revertendi, salvo praescripto can. 93.

Before the Code, the ancient and time honored axiom "*Omnis res per quascumque causas nascitur, per easdem dissolvitur,*" was employed by canonists to determine how a domicile might be lost.[1] To acquire a domicile, actual residence in a place and the intention of remaining there permanently were required. In virtue of the above mentioned axiom, both elements had to cease that the domicile be actually lost. Therefore, to lose a domicile one must actually depart with the intention of not returning. As in the acquisition, so in the loss of domicile both were simultaneously necessary.

Since the advent of the new method of acquiring a domicile, introduced by the Code, viz., by residence alone, this axiom is no longer universally true. If it were, it would follow that the domicile acquired by ten years' residence without the intention of remaining, would be lost by an absence of ten years, even though one had the intention of returning. According to the

[1] Sanchez, *De Matrimonio,* III, 23, 2; D'Angelo, *Il domicilio ecclesiastico,* pp. 29-30.

Code, however, simultaneous coincidence of actual departure and the intention of not returning are required that a domicile be lost, no matter how it is acquired.[2] It is not enough, therefore, to have the intention of departing, unless one actually departs from the place. Nor, on the other hand, is actual departure sufficient, unless it is accompanied by the intention of not returning.[3] It makes no difference which precedes, so long as both are present at the same time.

By the intention of not returning, be it noted, is meant the intention of not returning as an inhabitant, as an ordinary resident of the place. To acquire a domicile, it has been determined, the intention required is the intention of remaining in the place as an inhabitant—*more incolarum.* So, in a similar manner, to lose a domicile the intention required is the intention of never returning to the place as an inhabitant. On the other hand, this intention of not returning as an inhabitant is quite compatible with the intention of returning as a visitor. An example, perhaps, will best illustrate this principle. A seminarian, during the period of preparation for the priesthood, retains his parental domicile. His stay at the seminary is transient. He still retains the *"affectus domicilii apud parentes,"* and therefore, his parental home is still his domicile. When this seminarian is ordained, however, and receives his appointment he loses his parental domicile. He has begun a new and independent life,

---

[2] Canon 95; Cf. Chelodi, *Jus de Personis,* n. 94; Bouuaert-Simenon, *Manuale,* n. 248; *Epitome,* I, n. 187; Vidal, *Jus Canonicum,* II, n. 11.

[3] D'Annibale, *Summula,* I, n. 83, nota 14; S. R. Rota *in Causa Parisien,* 22 April 1913, *A.A.S.,* V (1913), p. 268.

and has given up the intention of ever coming back to live as an ordinary member in the family home, and this, there can be no doubt, constitutes the intention of not returning requisite for losing a domicile. This teaching has received confirmation in a decision of the Rota in a recent matrimonial case.[4] In this case, the Auditors of the Rota declared that the parental domicile of a certain young man had been lost, because the young man in question had intended never to return there *"ut ibi iterum perpetuo maneat."* He had, indeed, visited his parents' home on different occasions, but his intention, on the occasion of those visits, was not that of considering this home as his domicile in the canonical sense.[5]

Although it is certain that one is entirely free to abandon his domicile, the loss of a domicile is a fact that the law will not freely admit. A domicile once constituted is regarded in canon law as an acquired right—*a res favorabilis.*[6] It enjoys the favor of law, and hence its loss is considered to be a *res odiosa* and strictly to be interpreted. In virtue of this principle the domicile once acquired is not considered to be lost, until the contrary is clearly proved. The domicile is in possession, and in cases of doubt the presumption is in favor of its retention. Therefore even though one

[4] S. R. Rota, *in Causa Ravennaten,* 29 Dec. 1911—*A.A.S.,* IV, pp. 331 ff.

[5] S. R. Rota, *in Causa Ravennaten, l. c.*: "Exclusus erat animus redeundi Romam (paternum domicilium), ut ibi iterum perpetuo maneat; tempore visitationum . . . longe vero aberat ab eo animus seu intentio considerandi Roman (paternum domicilium) ut suum domicilium in sensu canonico."

[6] S. Romana Rota *in Causa Gratianopolitana,* 8 April 1913—*Decisiones Coram Lega,* dec. XXXVI, n. 13. S. R. Rota *in Causa Parisien,* 26 April 1916—*A.A.S.,* VIII (1916), 374.

has been absent for many years, his domicile is considered to exist until it is clearly proved that he has actually left with the certain intention of abandoning his domicile, never to return. In the past, especially in connection with cases involving the validity of marriages, the Auditors of the Rota have fully accepted and put into practice the above mentioned principles.[7]

In connection with the loss of domicile, mention must be made of a famous fragment of Roman law, the *lex "Ea quae,"* [8] which declares that "an engaged woman does not lose her domicile before the marriage has been contracted."[9] This very practical regulation has been received into Canon law, and has formed the basis of many decisions of the Roman Rota in cases concerning the validity of marriages attacked on the score of clandestinity.[10]

Briefly, the meaning of the law is that when an engaged woman leaves her domicile, and goes to reside, for example, in the parish of her intended husband, there to enter the marriage ceremony, she is not considered to have lost her original domicile until the marriage actually takes place. If, for some reason, the marriage does not take place, the woman is considered

[7] S. R. Rota *in Causa Gratianopolitana,* 17 July, 1912—*Dec. S. R. Rotae,* dec. XXXI, n. 4, 9. S. R. Rota *in Causa Gratianopolitana,* 8 April 1913—*Decisiones Coram Lega,* dec. XXXVI, n. 13; S. R. Rota *in Causa Parisien,* 22 April 1913—*A.A.S.,* V (1913), 268; S. R. Rota *in Causa Parisien,* 4 March 1916—*A.A.S.,* VIII (1916), 369-370.

[8] D. L. 1. 32.

[9] "Ea quae desponsa est, ante contractas nuptias non mutat domicilium."

[10] S. R. Rota *in Causa Parisien,* 5 May 1914—*A.S.S.,* VI (1914) 397 ff. "Quae juris Romani dispositio (1. Ea quae), ipso jure naturali innixa, viget etiam in jure canonico, et ab H.S.T. applicata fuit in Parisien nullit. Matrim, 27 July 1912." Cf. also S. R. Rota *in Causa Mohilien,* 18 April 1916—*A.A.S.,* VIII (1916), p. 415.

to have retained her former domicile.[11] The reason for this law is founded on the fact that the intention of the engaged woman in leaving her domicile is only conditional, viz., if the marriage takes place. If the marriage does not take place she will return to her parents' home.[12] Two points are to be especially noted in connection with this law. In the first place, there is question only of an engaged woman leaving her domicile in view of her approaching marriage. Secondly, this law must not be understood in the sense that an engaged woman, who has attained her majority, cannot change her domicile. There is no reason why a woman cannot use her right to change her domicile because she is engaged; she may do so for reasons quite unconnected with her coming marriage. All the law states is that if the change of domicile is due to the coming marriage, the possession of the original domicile remains unchanged.[13]

Article II—Loss of Quasi-Domicile

It is not clear just how a quasi-domicile was lost before the publication of the Code. Canonists, generally, apprehended the quasi-domicile as an extension, an imitation of the domicile—a sort of attenuated

[11] S. R. Rota *in Causa Parisien,* 5 May 1914—*A.A.S.,* VI (1914), pp. 397-8.

[12] S. R. Rota *in Causa Parisien,* 5 May 1914—*A.A.S.,* VI (1914), p. 397. "Derelictio domicilii ex parte sponsae . . . et incoepta habitatio in loco domicilio sponsi, factae sunt sub conditione, scilicet, quod matrimonium fiat: conditiones non impletae, prefata omnia jure nulla et irrita fiunt."

[13] S. R. R. *in Causa Parisien,* 5 May 1914—*A.A.S.,* VI, p. 398; Cf. Fourneret, *Le Domicile Matrimonial,* p. 53; Vidal, *Jus Canonicum,* II, n. 11, nota 5.

domicile.[14] As a result of this conception, they applied to the quasi-domicile, *servatis servandis,* the principles governing the domicile. Logically, then, applying the axiom used in connection with the loss of domicile,[15] one would expect them to declare that the quasi-domicile was lost by actual departure with the intention of not returning for over six months. Actually, however, most canonists merely declare that a quasi-domicile is lost by actual departure with the intention of not returning.[16] Only two writers explicitly discuss the question. One of them, V. Meysztowicz, who has written since the Code,[17] declares that in the old legislation a quasi-domicile was lost by departure with the intention of not returning for the same time as was required to constitute a domicile, i. e., for the greater part of a year. Unfortunately, however, he does not cite a single authority in favor of his statement. Another canonist, H. Gasparri,[18] who wrote before the Code, declares that authorities say nothing, at least explicitly, on the point. He admits that the axiom, *"Omnis res per quascumque causas nascitur, per easdem dissolvitur,"* applies to the loss of quasi-domicile. He is not certain, however, of the exact application and, as a result, expresses the desire that the ecclesiastical authorities proffer a decision on the point. Finally it is not improbable that the many prominent canonists including

[14] Cf. Langonio, Votum—*Anal. Eccl.,* vol. XIII (1905), pp. 380 ff; Chelodi, *Jus de Personis,* n. 92.

[15] Cf. page 143.

[16] D'Annibale, *Summula,* I, n. 84; Alberti, *Il domicilio ecclesiastico,* p. 35.

[17] Cf. *Jus Pontificum,* VI (1926), p. 49.

[18] *De domicilio et quasi-domicilio,* n. 66.

Gasparri,[19] D'Annibale,[20] and Wernz,[21] who denied the possibility of the simultaneous possession of two voluntary quasi-domiciles, at least implicitly acknowledged that a quasi-domicile was lost by departure with the intention of not returning for over six months.[22]

Happily, the Code has removed all uncertainty on the point. The quasi-domicile is lost in the same way as the domicile, i. e., by actual departure with the intention of not returning. Therefore, if a person left the place of his domicile with the intention of returning again, no absence, however long, will destroy his quasi-domicile. The law makes no distinction between the loss of domicile and quasi-domicile, and according to the well-known rule of law "*ubi lex non distinquit, nec nos distinguere debemus.*" The opinion of some canonists,[23] therefore, who declare that, under the present discipline, a quasi-domicile is lost by an absence of over six months is entirely devoid of probability. The words of the Code are eminently clear. It may be mentioned also that in the canon of the Schema of the Code to which the present canon corresponds it was stated that "a quasi-domicile was lost by an absence of six months."[24] The fact that these words were expunged is a clear and unmistakable indication of the mind of the legislator.

Finally, although the quasi-domicile enjoys the same favor of law as the domicile regarding its retention in

---

[19] *De Matrimonio*, n. 916.

[20] *Summula*, I, n. 84, nota 23.

[21] *Jus Decretalium*, IV, n. 139, nota 29.

[22] Cf. H. Gasparri, *l. c.*

[23] Cf. Augustine, *A Commentary*, vol. II, p. 15.

[24] Cf. Maroto, *Institutiones*, I, n. 413, nota 3.

cases of doubt, being a less slender bond than the domicile, it is more easily lost.[25]

What has been said thus far, applies only to the loss of the voluntary domicile and quasi-domicile. The loss of the legal domicile will be discussed when treating of the legal domicile in general.[26]

---

[25] S. R. Rota *in Causa Ravennaten,* 15 May, 1911—*A.A.S.,* III (1911), 487.

[26] Cf. Chapter IX.

CHAPTER VIII

PLURALITY OF DOMICILES AND QUASI-DOMICILES

Article I—Plurality of Domiciles

It was an express principle of Roman law that a person could have more than one domicile.[1] This principle was officially recognized in Canon law by Boniface VIII in the famous chapter *"Is qui,"*[2] and continued up to the Code as the common and certain teaching.[3] Although the Code does not expressly treat the question, it is quite certain that the principle of a plurality of domiciles obtains its full force under the new legislation. This principle is evidently implied in canon 1216, which states that a person can have many proper parishes. Canon 20 removes all doubt on the point. In this canon it is stated that if there is no express prescription of law, whether general or particular, covering a certain matter, a norm is to be taken . . . from the practice of the Roman Curia and from the common and constant teaching of doctors. But both the practice of the Roman Curia and the unanimous teaching of canonists before and after the Code

[1] D. L. 1. 5; D. L. 1. 6 § 2; D. L. 1. 27 § 2.

[2] C. 2., *de sepult,* III, 12 in VI°.

[3] D'Annibale, *Summula,* I, §84, nota 23; Alberti, *De domicilio ecclesiastico,* n. 5; D'Angelo, *Il domicilio ecclesiastico,* p. 24 ff.; H. Gasparri, *De domicilio et quasi-domicilio,* n. 22.

have admitted and accepted the principle of a plurality of domiciles.[4] The conclusion is obvious.

In their exposition of this principle canonists have commonly taught that in order to acquire a domicile in more than one place it is necessary to establish oneself more or less equally in each place. A strict mathematical equality is not necessary, they declare, as if one could not reside a little longer in one place than in another. On the contrary, the equality is to be taken morally, so that one dwell in whatever place a great, though not an equal part of the year.[5] This teaching is true of the origin of a plurality of domiciles, and it indicates, at the same time, the normal way in which they are retained and continued. It is not necessary, however, for the continuance of these domiciles that at each moment a person shall be prepared to dwell in or even retain his homes for equal terms of succeeding years. If some unforeseen cause should compel him to depart from one of his homes, even on the next day after its acquisition, he will retain his domicile there until, together with the intention of remaining, the actual habitation also ceases.[6]

The *"casus classicus"* of a plurality of domiciles is

---

[4] S. R. Rota *in Causa Ravennaten,* 15 May, 1911—*A.A.S.,* III (1911), 487. S. R. Rota *in Causa Gratianopolitana,* 17 July 1912—*Decisiones S. R. Rotae,* vol. IV, dec. XXXI, n. 4; S. R. R. *in Causa Gratianopolitana,* 8 April 1913, in *Decisiones Coram Lega,* dec. XXXVI, n. 5; Schmalzgrueber, lib. II, tit. II, n. 13; D'Annibale, *l. c.;* Wernz, *Jus Decretalium,* IV, n. 177, nota 190; *Epitome,* I, n. 183; Chelodi, *Jus de Personis,* n. 92; and authors passim.

[5] Schmalzgrueber, *l. c.;* D'Angelo, *l. c.;* H. Gasparri, *l. c.;* Chelodi, *l. c.;* De Meester, *Compendium,* I, n. 316.

[6] Schmalzgrueber, lib. II, tit. II, n. 9; Ojetti, *Commentarium,* II, pp. 50-51, nota 46; De Meester, *l. c.*

that of a person who establishes himself equally in two places. This case is admitted by all authors.[7]

Two questions now present themselves. Is it possible for a person to have more than two domiciles at the same time? Just how many domiciles can a person have at the same time? The possibility of having more than two domiciles at the same time was a principle defended by many canonists who wrote before the Code,[8] and admitted by a correspondingly great number of canonists who have written since the Code.[9]

Henry Gasparri discusses this question at some length in his work *De domicilio et quasi-domicilio.* According to him the Roman law gave an affirmative answer to the question as to whether or not a man could have more than two domiciles at the same time.[10] Gasparri's argument is that since there is no text in canon law which decides this question, recourse must be had to the Roman law; hence even for canon law an affirmative answer may be given.[11] In a recent case decided by the Sacred Congregation of the Council[12] this teach-

---

[7] D'Annibale, *Summula,* I, n. 84, nota 2; Alberti, *l. c.;* Wernz, *l. c.;* Maroto, *Institutiones,* I, n. 410; De Meester, *l. c.*

[8] Baldus, *Lectura Super Decret.,* lib. I, tit. III, C. 29, n. 3; Wiestner, lib. II, tit. II, n. 28; Schmalzgrueber, lib. II, tit. II. n. 13; H. Gasparri, *De domicilio et quasi-domicilio,* n. 22; Fourneret, *Le Domicile Matrimonial,* p. 109; Deshayes, *Questions Pratique sur le Mariage,* q. 24.

[9] Chelodi, *Jus de Personis,* n. 92; *Epitome,* I, n. 183; Vidal, *Jus Canonicum,* II, n. 13; Cappello, *De Matrimonio,* n. 683; Bouuaert-Simenon, *Manuale,* n. 242.

[10] D. L. 1. 5. Cf. H. Gasparri, *De domicilio et quasi-domicilio,* n. 22.

[11] H. Gasparri, *l. c.* Schmalzgrueber and Laurin also allege the authority of the Roman law.

[12] S. C. C. *in Causa Parisien,* 28 July 1906—*Thesaurus Resolut. S. C. C.* 165, 882 ff.

ing of Gasparri was referred to as "*verissima ac tutissima doctrina.*"

In answer to the question—how many domiciles can a person have at the same time—it is very difficult, speculatively speaking, to set a hard and fast rule. A number of canonists concede the possibility of possessing three domiciles at the same time,[13] while another group of canonists admit that four domiciles can be had at the same time.[14] Since the equality of establishment or residence in the different domiciles is to be taken morally, there seems to be no reason why a person cannot have three or four domiciles at the same time, by residing about three or four months in each.[15] In addition the domicile has always been regarded by the Roman Congregations as a *res favorabilis* and hence its acquisition should be widely and favorably, rather than strictly, interpreted.[16] In practice, therefore, it would seem quite probable that a person could have three or at most four domiciles at the same time.[17] It would seem also that the venturesome spirit who would have more than four domiciles might find himself in the strange and unenviable position of a *vagus.*

---

[13] Deshayes, *l. c.;* Vidal, *l. c.; Epitome, l. c.;* Cappello, *l. c.*

[14] Baldus, *l. c.;* Wiestner, *l. c.;* H. Gasparri, *l. c.;* Fourneret, *l. c.;* Chelodi, *l. c.;* Kinane, "Domicile in the New Code," *I. E. R.*, 5 Series, vol. XII, p. 225.

[15] Chelodi, *l. c.;* H. Gasparri, *l. c.*

[16] S. C. C. *in Causa Parisien,* 28 July 1906—*Thesaurus Resolut. S.C.C.* t. 165, pp. 882, ff. "Reapse quod quis habeat domicilium, imo plura quam unum domicilium est res favorabilis, et huic eam multo magis debemus ampliare quam restringere, potissimum in jure nostro, in quo considerantur domicilium et quasi domicilium in ordine ad exercenda jura et officia Christiana." S. R. Rota *in Causa Gratianopolitana,* 8 April 1913—*Decisiones Coram Lega,* dec. XXXVI, n. 13.

[17] Gasparri, *l. c.;* Chelodi, *l. c.*

Article II.—Plurality of Quasi-Domiciles

Before the Code it was quite freely admitted that a man could have a voluntary quasi-domicile and a legal quasi-domicile at the same time.[18] Authorities, however, were sharply divided as to whether or not a person could have two voluntary quasi-domiciles at the same time.

The opinion denying the possibility of having two voluntary quasi-domiciles at the same time was regarded as the common and more probable opinion, and was defended by many eminent canonists.[19] The opinion affirming the possibility of having two quasi-domiciles at the same time, however, did not lack able defenders,[20] and was regarded as truly probable by the Auditors of the Rota in a recent matrimonial case presided over by Cardinal Lega.[21]

The Code has not explicitly settled the question and recourse must be had to the prevailing teaching of canonists.

All canonists admit that a quasi-domicile acquired by residence alone can coexist with a quasi-domicile

---

[18] Wernz, *Jus Decretalium,* IV, n. 139, nota 29; Alberti, *De domicilio ecclesiastico,* p. 8.

[19] Gasparri, *de Matr.,* n. 916; D'Annibale, *Summula,* I, n. 84, nota 23; Wernz, *l. c.;* Ojetti, *Synopsis,* n. 1882; Alberti, *l. c.;* Deshayes, *o. c.,* q. 26.

[20] Boudinhon, *Quelques reflexions sur le domicile,* Can. Contemp., XXII, p. 273; Fourneret, *Le Domicile Matrimonial,* p. 134; H. Gasparri, *o. c.,* n. 54; De Becker, *De Spons. et Matr.,* n. 93; Wouters, *Comm. in Decr. Ne Temere,* app. III, p. 91.

[21] S. R. Rota *in Causa Wladislavien,* 7 Dec. 1912—*Decisiones Coram Lega,* dec. XXIX, n. 8; "Omnibus perpensus, concludere fas est . . . sententiam duo quasi-domicilia admittentem esse vere *probabilem et gravem.*"

acquired by residence and intention.[22] The controversy, however, arises anew when there is question of the coexistence of two quasi-domiciles acquired by residence and intention. While the majority of canonists affirm the possibility of simultaneously possessing two quasi-domiciles constituted by residence and intention, not a few deny this possibility.

Maroto,[23] who defends the affirmative opinion, bases his conclusions on the principle enunciated in Canon 95, namely, "A quasi-domicile is lost only when one leaves it with the intention of not returning." Maroto then argues: if a person, having a quasi-domicile in one place, betakes himself to another place intending to reside there for the greater part of the year, with the intention, however, of returning afterwards to the first place, this person retains his first quasi-domicile by virtue of Canon 95, and by virtue of Canon 92 he acquires also a second quasi-domicile.

Maroto then appeals to the reading of Canon 95 as it appeared in the Schema of the New Code. Before the final redaction, in the canon of the Schema which corresponded to the present canon 95, the following regulation appeared: "*Quasi domicilium autem amittitur quoque discessione a loco per sex menses completos, non obstante revertendi animo.*" The expunging of this latter prescription, Maroto claims, is an implicit confirmation of his opinion.[24] This opinion has enlisted the authority of the great majority of present day commentators.[25]

[22] Cf. *Epitome,* I, n. 184; Vidal, *Jus Canonicum,* II, n. 13; Bouuaert-Simenon, *Manuale,* n. 244.

[23] *Institutiones,* I, n. 413.

[24] Maroto, *l. c.*

[25] Maroto, *l. c.;* Ojetti, *Commentarium,* II, p. 50, nota 46; Chelodi, *Jus de Personis,* n. 92; Muniz, *Derecho Parroquial,* I, n. 82; Bouua-

Vermeersch,[26] who vigorously defends the negative opinion, disagrees entirely with the conclusion proposed by Maroto. In the example offered by Maroto, Vermeersch declares that he who leaves his quasi-domicile with the intention of dwelling in another place for the greater part of the year, retains neither the fact of residence, since he had departed; nor the intention of remaining, since one cannot at the same time wish to remain for the greater part of the year in two places during the same year. "Moreover," continues Vermeersch, "the intention of returning to the first quasi-domicile, or the intention of dwelling successively in two places for the greater part of the year, is the intention of recovering the quasi-domicile lost by departure or of having successively two quasi-domiciles." This opinion is also defended by Vidal[27] and De Meester.[28]

The arguments of Vermeersch do not appear to be convincing. He seems to exaggerate the conditions required for the continuance of the quasi-domicile. In the first place, although the fact of residence is necessary to secure a domicile, and is, at the same time, the normal way in which it is continued, it is not absolutely necessary for its continuance.[29] Therefore, if on the

---

ert-Simenon, *l. c.;* Coronata, *Institutiones,* I, n. 127; Toso, *Commentarium,* II, p. 24; Cocchi, *Commentarium,* II, p. 22; Roberti, *De Processibus,* I, n. 65; Vlaming, *Prael. de Matr.,* I, n. 68; Damen, *Theologia Moralis,* I, n. 149, nota 6; D'Angelo, *Jus Digestorum,* I, n. 428.

[26] *Epitome,* I, n. 185.

[27] *Jus Canonicum,* II, n. 14.

[28] *Compendium,* I, 319.

[29] Schmalzgrueber, lib. II, tit. II, n. 9. "ut domicilium [vel quasi-domicilium] jam acquisitum retineatur, non opus est, ut qui aliud habeat, semper ibidem habitat, sed potest quandoque . . . discedere,

very day after a quasi-domicile is secured one is compelled to depart for a good period of time, he will retain his quasi-domicile until actual departure is accompanied by the intention of not returning. Canon 95 is decisive on the point.[30]

In regard to the intention, it must be admitted that one cannot intend, at the same time, to reside for the greater part of the year in two places during the same year. But such an intention is not necessary in order that an individual simultaneously possess two quasi-domiciles. The intention must not necessarily be referred to one year, to this or to that year. All the Code requires is a generic intention of remaining for at least the greater part of the year. One may, for example, intend to reside in a place for five years.[31] Perhaps an example will serve to answer more clearly Vermeersch's objection. A young man matriculates at a university in New York City to begin his law studies. Desirous of pursuing a special course at a university in Philadelphia during the following year, he leaves New York with the intention of returning later to complete his studies. Vermeersch certainly would admit that the young man has acquired a quasi-domicile in New York. Has he lost it by going to Philadelphia? Canon 95 declares that a quasi-domicile is lost by actual depar-

---

modo animum redcundi habeat . . . quia non omne quod requiritur ad constitutionem actus, portinus etiam requiritur ad ejus conservationem."

[30] Cf. Ojetti, *l. c.*

[31] S. R. Rota *in Wladislavien,* 7 Dec. 1912—*Dec. Coram Lega, l. c.* "Et revera considerari debet quasi-domicilium quatenus se extendere potest ad plures annos et tunc facile considerantur casus in quibus necessario consistere videntur duo quasi-domicilia." Cf. Ojetti, *l. c.;* Bouuaert-Simenon, *l. c*

ture with the intention of not returning. But this young man has the intention of returning. Therefore he retains his quasi-domicile in New York. Does he acquire a quasi-domicile in Philadelphia? Canon 92 declares that a quasi-domicile is acquired by residence in a place with the intention of remaining for the greater part of the year. The young man in question intends to reside there for a year. Therefore, he acquires a quasi-domicile in Philadelphia. He has, therefore, two quasi-domiciles acquired by residence and intention, and their possession is fully protected, as we have seen, by the law.[32]

Finally, Vermeersch, at least implicitly, seems to be of the opinion that a quasi-domicile is lost by the intention of staying away for a period of more than six months. He says, "The intention of returning to the first quasi-domicile is the intention of recovering the quasi-domicile lost by departure or of having successively two quasi-domiciles."[33] Such an opinion is entirely opposed to Canon 95.

As matters now stand, it would seem that the opinion affirming the possibility of a plurality of voluntary quasi-domiciles acquired by residence and intention, is speculatively, at least more probable, if not certain.[34] This opinion, therefore, can be safely followed in practice.

---

[32] Cf. Ojetti, *l. c.;* Maroto, *l. c.*

[33] *Epitome,* I, n. 185.

[34] Ojetti, *l. c.;* Maroto, *l. c.*

CHAPTER IX

LEGAL OR NECESSARY DOMICILE AND QUASI-DOMICILE

Article I.—The Legal or Necessary Domicile

Canon 93, §1.—Uxor, a viro legitime non separata, necessario retinet domicilium viri sui; amens, domicilium curatoris; minor, domicilium illius cujus potestate subjicitur.

The necessary domicile, which traces its origin to the Roman law,[1] and which was accepted in general by canonical jurisprudence,[2] is formally acknowledged for the first time in Canon law by the New Code.[3]

The Code does not define the legal domicile; it merely enumerates those upon whom this domicile is conferred. The generally accepted definition of canonists[4] which has been received by the Roman Congregations,[5] is that the legal domicile is that which is necessarily acquired by disposition of law.

[1] D. L. 1. 22 § 1, 3, 6; D. L. 1, 38 § 3; C. X. 40 (39) 9; D. L. 1. 23 § 1.

[2] Passerini, *Comm. in Sexto,* c. cum nullus, n. 3; Schmalzgrueber, lib. II, tit. II, n. 14; D'Annibale, *Summula,* I, n. 83; Alberti, *De domicilio ecclesiastico,* n. 5; S. R. Rota *in Causa Ravennaten,* 15 May 1911, *A.A.S.,* III (1911), p. 487.

[3] Canon 93 § 1.

[4] Alberti, *De domicilio ecclesiastico,* n. 5; D'Angelo, *Il domicilio ecclesiastico,* p. 35 ff.; Wernz, *Jus Decretalium,* IV, n. 177, nota 190; *Epitome,* I, n. 183; Chelodi, *Jus de Personis,* n. 92; Vidal, *Jus Canonicum,* II, 12.

[5] S. R. Rota *in Causa Ravennaten,* 15 May 1911—*A.A.S.,* III (1911), p. 487; S. R. Rota *in Causa Parisien,* 27 Jan. 1912—*A.A.S.,* IV (1912), 277.

This domicile is acquired independently of intention or residence, or both. It matters not whether the person actually resides in the place, or whether he has the positive intention of not residing there; he has a domicile nevertheless, a domicile conferred by operation of law, a *domicilium legale, necessarium.*[6] By the same disposition of law this domicile is necessarily retained, as long as the state or condition to which it is annexed endures; and it does not cease until that state or condition is legitimately lost.[7] It must be remembered, however, that although this necessary domicile *as such* ceases upon the cessation of the fact upon which it was founded, it is presumed to have passed into a voluntary domicile unless it is clear that it has been definitely abandoned.[8] Thus, for example, a son upon reaching his majority loses his necessary domicile *as a necessary domicile,* but he is presumed to retain it as a voluntary domicile until it is clear that he has given it up. From what has been said it is

---

[6] In the different cases the law itself supplies the lack of intention or residence. Cf. Wernz, *Jus Decretalium,* IV, n. 177, nota 190, "In casu legis dispositio supplet defectum habitationis vel intentionis;" D'Angelo, *Il domicilio ecclesiastico,* pp. 35-36; Ojetti, *Commentarium,* II, p. 54, nota 9.

[7] Alberti, *De domicilio ecclesiastico,* p. 9; "Ammittitur vero domicilium necessarium, statim ac cessat factum, quod requiritur tamquam conditio, ut lex aut legislatoris voluntas servetur." S. R. Rota *in Causa Ravennaten,* 15 May, 1911—*A.A.S.,* III (1911), 483, ff.

[8] S. R. Rota *in Causa Ravennaten,* 15 May 1911—*A.A.S.,* III (1911), 487, "Domicilium necessarium censeretur transire in voluntarium, et tamdiu retineri praesumeretur, quam diu non constaret, illi, expresse vel tacite, directe vel indirecte, fuisse renuntiatum." Cf. Feije, *De imp. et disp. Matrim.,* n. 204; Alberti, *l. c.,* Bouuaert-Simenon, *Manuale juris canonici,* n. 245.

evident that the legal or necessary domicile is a fiction of law.[9]

Canon 93 mentions three classes of persons upon whom a legal or necessary domicile is conferred, viz., married women, minors and those deprived of the use of reason.

Married Women. That the married woman acquired and necessarily retained the domicile of her husband was a principle enunciated by the Roman law,[10] accepted by canonists generally,[11] and confirmed by the practice of the Roman Congregations.[12] The Code in Canon 93 retains this principle. "The married woman necessarily retains the domicile of her husband, unless she is legitimately separated from him." This regulation flows from the very nature of the married state, whose right ordering demands a community of bed and board. This obligation of cohabitation, founded in the nature of things, is imposed also by the new law in Canon 1128.[13]

[9] Carnelluti, "Note critiche intorno ai concetti di domicilio, residenza, etc.," *Archivio Giuridico,* Vol. LXXV (1905), p. 430 ff.; Ojeti, *l. c.* "De jure . . . dantur . . . domicilia fictitia, quae constituuntur ex fictione juris, quando scilicet quis in aliquo loco non habet verum domicilium, sive ibi commoretur vel non; sed hoc non obstante, jus ipsum eum habet tam quam vere ibidem domiciliatum."

[10] D. L. 1. 22 § 1; D. L. 1. 38 § 3.

[11] Panormitanus, c. conquestus, *de foro comp.,* n. 7; Pirhing, lib. II, tit. II, n. 11; D'Annibale, *Summula,* I, § 83, nota 16; Ojetti, *Synopsis Rerum Moralium,* n. 1870; Alberti, *De domicilio ecclesiastico,* n. 5.

[12] S. R. Rota *in Causa Wladislavien,* 7 Dec. 1912—*Decisiones Coram Lega,* dec. XXIX, n. 6; S. R. Rota *in Causa Gratianopolitana,* 8 April 1913—*Decisiones Coram Lega,* dec. XXXVI, n. 11; "Uxor et filii habent domicilium legale necessarium apud patrem;" S. R. Rota *in Causa Parisien,* 4 March 1916—*A.A.S.,* VIII (1916), 367 ff.

[13] Canon 1128: "Conjuges servare debent vitae conjugalis communionem, nisi justa causa eos excuset."

The general rule, that the wife necessarily retains the domicile of the husband, suffers an exception in the event of legitimate separation. Previous to the publication of the Code it was the common teaching that besides the case of legitimate separation, the wife did not necessarily retain the domicile of her husband in the event of malicious desertion.[14] Whatever doubt may have existed regarding the application of this regulation under the Code has been dispelled by a decision of the Pontifical Commission for the interpretation of the canons of the Code given on July 22, 1922. The question was asked: "Whether a wife, who has been maliciously deserted by her husband, can, in accordance with canon 93 §2, acquire a distinct domicile of her own?" The reply was "In the negative, unless she has obtained from an ecclesiastical judge a perpetual separation, or a separation for an indefinite period."[15] The words of the decision are clear and need little comment. It may be noted that if a wife is maliciously deserted, she may *lawfully* live apart from her husband, but she cannot acquire a domicile, unless a sentence is passed.[16]

In addition to this case, a wife may lawfully separate from her husband, and thus be free to acquire her own domicile, in virtue of certain causes determined in Canons 1130 and 1131.

According to Canon 1130, in the event that one of

---

[14] Instruction of S. C. de Prop. Fide, 1883—*Collectanea S. D. P. F.*, n. 1573, art. 2; *Austrian Instruction* § 96—*Collectio Lacensis* V, 1293 ff.; Gasparri, *De Matrimonio*, n. 1168; Mansella, *De Imped. Matrim.*, p. 174; Lega, *De Judiciis*, I, n. 340; Wernz, *Jus Decretalium*, V, n. 286.

[15] Pontif. Comm. Inter. Cod., 22 July, 1922—*A.A.S.*, XIV (1922), 526.

[16] *Epitome*, I, n. 183.

the spouses is guilty of adultery, the innocent party may legitimately depart, either in virtue of a judicial sentence or on his or her own initiative. Adultery, it may be noted, gives the innocent party the right to a perpetual separation.

According to Canon 1131, if one party joins a non-Catholic sect; if he leads a criminal or despicable life; if he threatens great bodily or spiritual danger to the other party; or if through cruelties, or in any other way, he makes the common life too difficult, the other party may legitimately leave the guilty party. The separation in this case should ordinarily be done with the intervention of the local Ordinary; it may also be done on one's own initiative, if the cause for separation is certain and there is danger in delay. In cases of separation for causes other than adultery the separation is conditioned on the continuance of the cause of separation. If the cause ceases, the parties are obliged to resume the marital life.

Applying these principles the following conclusions may be stated.

In the event of separation by reason of adultery, there is no difficulty. Adultery is a cause for perpetual separation, and whether the wife separates on her own authority or that of the Ordinary she can immediately acquire a domicile. Canon 1130 is decisive on the point.

In the event of separation for the causes enumerated in Canon 1131, a distinction must be made. If the separation is for a certain definite period, obviously the wife cannot acquire a domicile, since she cannot have the intention of permanent residence. If the separation is for an indefinite time, by an analogy with the decree of the Pontifical Commission in connection with the case of malicious desertion,[17] it would seem that she can acquire a domicile.

According to the second section of Canon 93, a married woman, not legitimately separated from her husband, can acquire a proper quasi-domicile. The silence of the Code in regard to a voluntary domicile is a clear indication that the wife, under these circumstances, cannot acquire one. The fact that she is permitted to acquire one when lawfully separated places the matter beyond all shadow of doubt.[18]

Minors. "A minor necessarily retains the domicile of the person to whom he is subject."[19] In Roman law a different principle obtained. The minor (*filiusfamilias*) did not necessarily retain the domicile of his father.[20] The early canonists followed the Roman law and it was not until the eighteenth century that the present teaching came into prominence.[21] On the eve of the Code, the law as it now stands was the unanimous opinion of canonists,[22] confirmed by the practice of the Roman Curia.[23]

---

[17] Pontif. Comm. Inter. Cod. 22 July 1922—*A.A.S.*, XIV (1922), 526. Cf. above page 163.

[18] Vidal, *Jus Canonicum*, II, n. 13; *Epitome*, I, § 185; Bouuaert-Simenon, *Manuale juris canonici*, n. 245.

[19] Canon 93, § 1.

[20] D. L. 1. 6. § 1. "Filius civitatem, exua pater ejus naturalem originem ducit, non domicilium sequitur." Glossa on D. L. 1. 6; Bartolus, in D. L. 1. 3. "Filiusfamilias potest sibi constituere domicilium"; Cujas, lib. I. Responsa Papinian.

[21] Cf. page 59.

[22] Gasparri, *De Matrimonio*, n. 925; D'Annibale, *Summula*, I, § 83, nota 17; Alberti, *De domicilio ecclesiastico*, n. 6; D'Angelo, *Il domicilio ecclesiastico*, p. 37.

[23] S. C. C. *in Causa Parisien*, 26 April 1902—*A.S.S.*, XXXIV, p. 660; S. C. C. *in Causa Parisien*, 18 July 1903—*Anal. Eccl.* XI, p. 286;

Although, before the Code, it was certain that a minor necessarily retained the domicile of his father or guardian, it was by no means certain at what age he ceased to be a minor. In the absence of any canonical provision, authorities were divided as to whether either the Roman law or the civil law was to be followed, or whether the regulation of Canon law regarding the impediment of age should provide a norm.[24] The Code has removed all difficulty on the point. In Canon 88 it is clearly stated that a minor is one who has not yet completed his twenty-first year of age. A child therefore necessarily retains the domicile of him to whose power he is subject until he reaches the age of twenty-one. After that time this domicile ceases to exist as a necessary domicile, but it is presumed that it is retained as a voluntary domicile until it is evident that it has been renounced.

In the event of the father's death, the minor necessarily retains the domicile of his mother. If both parents are dead the minor necessarily retains the domicile of his tutor or guardian.[25] Although the Code makes frequent mention of the guardian (*tutor-curator*), in no place does it prescribe any definite general rules concerning their appointment or qualifications. It would seem that a guardian appointed by civil law is not excluded. This may be inferred

---

S. R. Rota *in Causa Ravennaten,* 15 May 1911—*A.A.S.*, III (1911), 487; S. R. Rota *in Causa Parisien,* 27 Jan. 1912—*Decisiones S. R. Rotae,* vol. IV, dec. 6.

[24] Wernz, Votum—*Anal. Eccl.*, vol. VI (1899), n. 28; *Nouvelle Revue Theologique,* vol. XXIV, p. 663 ff.

[25] S. C. C. *in Causa Parisien,* 26 April 1902—*A.S.S.*, XXXIV, p. 660; Bouuaert-Simenon, *Manuale Juris Canonici,* n. 245; Maroto, *Institutiones,* I, n. 411; Chelodi, *Jus de Personis,* n. 92.

from a number of canons in the Code,[26] and from the common teaching of canonists.[27] In the absence, therefore, of any ecclesiastical regulation, the prescriptions of the civil law may safely be followed.[28]

According to the second section of Canon 93, a minor who has ceased to be an infant, i.e., has attained his seventh year,[29] can acquire a proper quasi-domicile. He cannot, however, acquire a proper domicile. This is clearly indicated by the silence of the Code on this point, and is confirmed by the practice of the Roman Congregations,[30] and by the teaching of commentators on the New Code.[31]

Insane Persons. "The insane person necessarily retains the domicile of his guardian (curator)." What has been said above regarding the tutor of the minor is to be applied also to the curator of the insane person. In the absence, therefore, of any ecclesiastical regulation, the civil law is to be followed.[32]

---

[26] Canons 1648 and 1650 in connection with Canon 1651.

[27] Maroto, *o. c.*, n. 441; Bouuaert-Simenon, *l. c.;* De Meester, *Compendium,* I, n. 317, nota 4; Augustine, *Commentary,* II, p. 12; Toso, *Commentarium,* II, p. 21.

[28] De Meester, *l. c.*, Bouuaert-Simenon, *l. c.*

[29] Canon 88 § 3.

[30] S. C. C. *in Causa Parisien,* 26 April 1920—*A.A.S.*, XXIV, p. 660. "Exploratum in jure est, filios minores nullum habere posse aluid domicilium quam illud patris, matris vel demum tutoris. Hoc principium communiter receptum fuit." S. R. Rota *in Causa Ravennaten,* 15 May 1911—*A.A.S.*, III (1911), 487.

[31] *Epitome,* I, n. 185; Chelodi, *Jus de Personis,* n. 92; "Hi omnes (uxor, amens, minor) . . . alterum domicilium proprium sibi obtinere nequeunt." Coronata, *Institutiones,* I, n. 126; Santamaria, *Commentarios al Codigo Canonico,* I, pp. 125-126.

[32] Cf. Maroto, *o. c.*, n. 441; De Meester, *Compendium,* I, n. 317, nota 4; Bouuaert-Simenon, *l. c.;* Toso, *l. c.*, *Apollinaris,* I (1928), p. 509.

In view of the second section of Canon 93 it is clear that the insane person, unlike the married woman and the minor, cannot acquire a proper quasi-domicile. Some canonists, indeed, are of the opinion that an insane person can acquire a quasi-domicile by actual residence in a place for the greater part of a year.[33] This opinion cannot be admitted. Not a single argument can be urged in its favor, and it is clearly opposed to a cardinal rule of interpretation as enunciated in Canon 18. This canon declares that laws are to be understood according to the proper signification of the words, considered in their text and context. A careful reading of section two of Canon 93 with a backward glance at section one reveals the unmistakable intention of the legislator to exclude insane persons from acquiring a quasi-domicile. In Canon 93, §1, wives, minors and insane persons are declared to have necessary domiciles. In the next breath, as it were, Canon 93, §2, permits wives and minors to acquire a quasi-domicile of their own. The logical conclusion is that insane persons cannot acquire a proper quasi-domicile.

This conclusion is strengthened by the fact that a quasi-domicile (even that constituted by actual residence) must be acquired by a personal action performed *humano modo*. The act by which a quasi-domicile is acquired must be a human act, for from involuntary and unconscious actions no juridical effect can follow, since those things which in law depend on one's own personal action and are not induced by a fiction of law, presuppose in the agent a reflection of the mind and the *voluntas agendi*. But insane per-

---

[33] De Meester, *l. c.*

sons are incapable of a human act, since they are deprived of the use of reason.[34] It must be concluded, therefore, that they cannot acquire a proper quasi-domicile.[35]

If the insane person has no guardian, or if his guardian is a *vagus*, it would seem that he must be placed in the category of *vagi*.[36]

The question now arises, is the enumeration in Canon 93, §1, taxative or demonstrative? Authorities are not agreed. A number of canonists[37] are of the opinion that the enumeration is demonstrative. Canon 93, §1, these writers claim, does not exhaust the list of those who have necessary domiciles. Others also have this kind of a domicile. The examples most frequently mentioned are those of religious and clerics. It is in connection with religious alone that any arguments for this opinion are advanced. Vermeersch,[38] the most prominent defender of this opinion, declares that religious after profession are non "sui juris," but are equivalent to minors. Since, therefore, they are incapable of acquiring a domicile of fact, a necessary domicile, by an analogy of law, must be given them. Appreciating the fact that the religious superior labors under the same incapacity, since he too is a religious, Vermeersch asserts that single religious par-

[34] Canon 88, § 3.

[35] Bouuaert-Simenon, *Manuale juris canonici*, n. 245. "Non videtur ratio declarandi infantes quoque et amentes acquirere quasi-domicilium, si de facto per sex menses in quodam loco commorantur." Santamaria, *o. c.*, pp. 125-126; Maroto, *Institutiones*, I, n. 412; Toso, *Commentarium*, II, p. 21.

[36] Cf. Farren, *Domicile and Quasi-Domicile*, p. 94.

[37] *Epitome*, I, n. 188; Ojetti, *Commentarium*, II, page 52, nota 3; Chelodi, *Jus de Personis*, n. 92; Maroto, *Institutiones*, I, n. 410.

[38] *Epitome*, *l. c.*

ticipate in the domicile of the moral person—the convent. This conclusion, according to Vermeersch, is founded in the old law and, by virtue of Canon 20, supplies a norm for the new law. This opinion is also defended by Vidal,[39] Chelodi,[40] Ojetti,[41] Maroto,[42] and others.[43]

Another group of Canonists declare that the enumeration of Canon 93, § 1, is taxative.[44] Kinane[45] regards the view of Vermeersch as untenable. In the first place, Kinane declares that this view is opposed to Canon 93, §1. According to this canon, only three classes of persons are mentioned as having necessary domiciles. Since neither here nor elsewhere in the Code is there a similar statement in regard to others the logical conclusion is that no other class has this species of domicile. Kinane then asserts that Vermeersch's theory is not in harmony with the recognized principles of interpretation; the words of Canon 93 in their text and context give a clear and definite meaning. It is, therefore, unjustifiable for a private interpreter, by reason of a mere analogy to give the law a more extended signification. Finally, argues Kinane, from the words *"professi domicilium necessarium obtinebant in loco conventus cui adscripti sunt,"* it would seem that Vermeersch applies his theory only to those permanently attached to some

[39] *Jus Canonicum,* II, n. 12, nota 10.

[40] *Jus de Personis,* n. 92.

[41] *Commentarium,* II, p. 52, nota 3.

[42] *Institutiones,* I, n. 410.

[43] Coronata, *Institutiones,* I, n. 128; Bouuaert-Simonen, *Manuale Juris Canonici,* n. 245.

[44] Kinane, *I.E.R.,* 5 Series, vol. XXVII (1926), pp. 647-8. Oesterle, *Comm. Pro Religiosis,* vol. V (1924), pp. 167 ff.

[45] *L. c.*

particular house. The term *ascriptio* implies the notion of permanence, and besides the extension of this theory to those who may be moved about from house to house at the will of the Superior seems repugnant on the face of it. But it is entirely unnecessary that those attached permanently to a house should be assigned a necessary domicile, since in the ordinary course of events they would have there a domicile of fact.[46].

Oesterle,[47] who also defends the taxative enumeration of Canon 93, establishes quite clearly that, with the exception of clerical religious who are ordained before the profession of temporary vows, religious *do not need any domicile.* The Code has made ample provision for them otherwise in regard to the exercise of all their rights and duties, e.g., in regard to the reception of the sacraments,[48] ecclesiastical burial,[49] and proper forum.[50] Oesterle then points out two places in which the Code implicitly denies that religious have a necessary domicile. In the first place, in connection with the competent forum for ecclesiastical trials, Canon 1561 declares that a proper forum is acquired by a domicile or a quasi-domicile. A little later, in Canon 1563, it is stated that a religious acquires a proper forum *"in loco domus suae."* If religious have a domicile, what need is there of this regulation, and why does the Code say *"in loco domus suae"*? Why does it not say *"in loco ubi religiosus domicilium habet"*?

---

[46] Kinane, *l. c.*

[47] Oesterle, *Comm. Pro Relig.*, V (1924), 167 ff.

[48] Cf. Canons 514, 518, 529, 956, 964, 965.

[49] Cf. canons 1208, 1221, 1222, 1224, 1230, §§ 3, 4, 5.

[50] Cf. Canons 1563, 1652, 1653, § 6.

Again, in connection with Ordination, Canon 965 prescribes that the bishop to whom a religious superior should send dimissorial letters is the bishop of the diocese in which the religious house is situated to which the religious belongs. Why, asks Oesterle, does not the Code say *"domus in qua ordinandus habet domicilium"*? [51] Clearly the Code does not acknowledge a *domicilium religiosorum.*

From what has been said, it would seem that the opinion of Vermeersch, declaring that religious have a necessary domicile, cannot be admitted. The arguments of Kinane and Oesterle are most convincing, while the arguments advanced by Vermeersch do not prove his contention. Vermeersch declares that religious participate in the domicile of the moral person—the convent. But a moral person has no domicile properly speaking.[52] The idea of domicile relates to the physical life of man, and is not therefore properly applicable to legal persons. Legal persons have, it may be said, something corresponding or similar to a domicile, a seat (*sedes*), but not a domicile in the true sense of the word and in the sense contemplated by law.[53]

Vermeersch also alleges that his opinion is founded on the old law.[54] The force of this argument can very properly be questioned. It is true that some canonists [55] immediately before the Code speak of a neces-

[51] Oesterle, *Comm. Pro. Relig.*, vol. V (1924), *l. c.*

[52] Laurin, Wesen und Bedeutung des Domicils—*Archiv für katholisches Kirchenrecht,* 26 (1871), § 10; Savigny, *System des Heutigen Römischen Rechts,* vol. VIII, § 354.

[53] Laurin, *l. c.*

[54] *Epitome,* I, § 188.

[55] Alberti, *De domicilio ecclesiastico,* n. 5; D'Angelo, *Il domicilio ecclesiastico,* p. 37.

sary domicile of religious, but the authorities they allege, viz., a gloss on the chapter "*Execrabilis*" of the *Extravagantes* of John XXII,[56] and the canonist Pirhing,[57] do not declare that religious have a necessary domicile. They state merely that a religious is considered (*censetur-reputatur*) to have a domicile in the monastery to which he is attached. In addition it may be mentioned that a necessary domicile—in fact any domicile for religious has never been officially recognized.

The defenders of the demonstrative enumeration of Canon 93 also declare that clerics possessing a residential benefice have a necessary domicile in the place of benefice. This necessary domicile cannot be admitted for the reason that there is no need for it. By virtue of Canon 956, candidates for orders must have a domicile in order to be licitly ordained, either by the bishop of the domicile (the *episcopus proprius*), or by another with dimissorial letters from the bishop of domicile. If these candidates are ordained for the diocese in which they have a domicile, they do not lose this domicile upon ordination; and since they have a voluntary, what need is there to give them a necessary domicile? If the candidates are ordained for another diocese in which they have no domicile, they will acquire a voluntary domicile in this diocese when they go to that diocese with the intention of entering upon a perpetual life work there, and hence with the intention of permanently staying there.[58] In this case, also, a necessary domicile is not needed.

Finally, in addition to the first two arguments of

[56] C. execrabilis, *de praebend.* in Extravag. Joannis, XXII.

[57] Lib. II, tit. II, n. 17.

[58] Cf. Canons 111, 112, 117.

Kinane,[59] the following consideration may be offered in opposing the existence of any legal domicile other than those mentioned by the Code. A legal domicile is a *fictio juris*. One of the cardinal rules in connection with the action of a fiction is that it cannot be extended from person to person.[60] It follows therefore that it would be unlawful to grant a legal domicile to any but those mentioned expressly in the law.[61]

As matters stand, it would seem that the opinion of those who declare the enumeration of Canon 83 to be taxative is the only true one.

Article II.—The Legal or Necessary Quasi-Domicile

The Code mentions only a legal domicile. Has the legal quasi-domicile also a place in the new legislation? Before the Code the legal quasi-domicile was generally admitted by canonists,[62] and acknowledged also by the officials of the Rota.[63] The Code, however, makes no mention of the legal quasi-domicile, and the silence of the Code has given rise to a sharp controversy on the point.

A number of canonists take for granted its existence

---

[59] Page 170.

[60] Menochius, *De Praesumptionibus*, lib. I, q. 8, n. 35; Reiffenstuel, lib. I, tit. II, n. 184; Roberti, *De Processibus*, vol. II, n. 376, p. 106, nota 1.

[61] Cf. Benedict XIV, *Ad Audientiam*, 15 Feb. 1753—*Fontes*, n. 424. "Fictio juris non habet locum nisi in casibus a jure expressis."

[62] Alberti, *De domicilio ecclesiastico*, n. 5; D'Angelo, *Il domicilio ecclesiastico*, pp. 35-36; Gasparri, *De Matrimonio*, n. 925.

[63] S. R. Rota *in Causa Ravennaten*, May 15, 1911 (1912)—*A.A.S.*, III (1911), 487 ff.; S. R. Rota *in Causa Parisien*, 27 Jan. 1912—*A.A.S.*, IV (1912), 277 ff.

in the new law without any qualification.[64] According to them a quasi-domicile is imposed by law in the same cases as the legal domicile. It is argued, in the first place, that the quasi-domicile is patterned after the domicile; it imitates, as it were, the domicile, and in law the quasi-domicile is on an equal footing with the domicile unless the opposite is clearly apparent.[65] Confirmation of this view is sought on the ground that, although the existence of the legal quasi-domicile is not stated in the law, it is acknowledged beyond shadow of doubt by present-day jurisprudence. In support of this statement, the defenders of this view allege a number of decisions of the Roman Rota, issued shortly before the publication of the Code.[66] It is asserted, finally, that the complete subjection of dependent persons to those under whose authority they are subject requires that these persons retain not only the domicile but also the quasi-domicile of the parent, husband, or guardian.[67]

Vermeersch,[68] while disagreeing in principle with the foregoing opinion, admits a legal quasi-domicile under certain circumstances. *Per se,* he declares, the legal quasi-domicile has no place in the new discipline. The silence of the Code is a voluntary, a positive silence. The exclusion of the legal quasi-domicile is more evident when it is remembered that wives and minors

---

[64] Chelodi, *Jus de Personis,* n. 92; Maroto, *Institutiones,* I, n. 413; Bouuaert-Simenon, *Manuale,* n. 245; Vidal, *Jus Canonicum,* II, n. 12; Damen, *Theologia Moralis,* I, n. 149, pp. 107-8, nota 6.

[65] Chelodi, *l. c.,* Bouuaert-Simenon, *l. c.*

[66] S. R. Rota *in Causa Ravennaten,* 15 May 1911—*A.A.S.,* III (1911), 487 ff.; S. R. Rota *in Causa Parisien,* 12 Jan. 1912—*A.A.S.,* IV (1912), 277, ff. Cf. Chelodi, *l. c.*

[67] Maroto, *l. c.,* Bouuaert-Simenon, *l. c.*

[68] *Epitome,* I, n. 185

can choose their own quasi-domicile. However, continues Vermeersch, if the husband or guardian has no domicile but only a quasi-domicile, and if further, these protected persons have no proper quasi-domicile, then, by applying the argument from analogy which Canon 20 permits, it must be said that they participate in the quasi-domicile of their husband or guardian lest they be said to be *vagi.*[69]

A third group of canonists[70] deny the existence of the legal quasi-domicile in the new legislation. Kinane,[71] who discusses the matter at some length, argues that in order that one may have a legal quasi-domicile it is necessary, as the name itself indicates, that it be assigned by law; but neither in Canon 93, which speaks of the legal domicile, nor anywhere else in the Code is there any mention of legal quasi-domicile. The legal quasi-domicile, therefore, has no place in the new legislation.[72] Kinane denies also the existence of the legal quasi-domicile even in the restricted sense advocated by Vermeersch. According to him, the argument of Vermeersch that, unless these dependent persons are give a legal quasi-domicile, they would be *vagi,* is not convincing. There is no difficulty in admitting they are *vagi. Vagi* are recognized and fully provided for in the Code. He continues, "If the

---

[69] *Epitome, l. c.*

[70] Ojetti, *Commentarium,* II, p. 50, nota 40; De Meester, *Compendium,* I, n. 318, nota 7; Toso, *Commentarium,* II, p. 21; Ayrinhac, *General Legislation,* n. 200; Kinane—*I.E.R.*, 5 Series, vol. 27 (1926), p. 81.

[71] *I.E.R.*, 5 Series, vol. 27, p. 81.

[72] Cf. Ojetti, *l. c.,* "In jure nostro unice admitti quasi domicilium *voluntarium;* quasi-domicilium *necessarium* non admittitur, quia de eo nulla est mentio in lege, quem admodum nulla est in praxi necessitas." Cf. also De Meester, *l. c.,* Toso, *l. c.*

legal position were that nobody could be without either a domicile or a quasi-domicile there would be solid grounds for Vermeersch's contention; as things stand now it is devoid of all probability." [73] Kinane concludes, "All must admit that dependent persons who have not acquired a quasi-domicile of their own are *vagi,* if the persons . . . upon whom they depend are *vagi.* What is the difficulty of admitting them to be *vagi* in the circumstances under consideration?" [74] This opinion is supported also by Ojetti,[75] De Meester,[76] Toso,[77] and Ayrinhac.[78]

Speculatively the opinion denying the existence of the legal quasi-domicile appears to be the truer. It is in absolute conformity with the clear words of the law and therefore with the apparent mind of the legislator. Again, the argument from the absolute silence of the Code, to which Kinane appeals and which Vermeersch admits, takes on greater force when it is recalled that the legislator was not unaware that the accepted opinion before the Code affirmed the existence of the legal quasi-domicile.

It cannot be denied, however, that the opposite opinion is solidly probable, in view especially of the practice of the Rota before the Code, and of the prominent authorities who have defended it since the Code.

[73] Kinane—*I.E.R., l. c.*
[74] Kinane—*I.E.R., l. c.*
[75] Ojetti, *l. c.*
[76] De Meester, *l. c.*
[77] Toso, *l. c.*
[78] Ayrinhac, *l. c.*

CHAPTER X

THE PLACE OF DOMICILE AND QUASI-DOMICILE

Canon 92, §3.—Domicilium vel quasi-domicilium in paroecia vel quasi paroecia dicitur *paroeciale;* in dioecsi, vicariatu, praefectura, non autem in paroecia vel quasi paroecia, *diocesanum.*

Before the publication of the Code, a controversy of no small moment existed concerning the exact place of the domicile and the quasi-domicile. By far the greater number of canonists acknowledged none but a parochial domicile.[1] A number of others, however, declared that one could have a domicile in a city, although not in any particular parish of that city.[2] These canonists appealed to the famous chapter *"Is qui"* of Boniface VIII,[3] which, they declared, had never been repealed.[4] Others, finally, advocated a purely diocesan domicile, i. e. a domicile in a diocese but not in any particular parish of that diocese.[5] This view received some added

[1] Gasparri, *De Matrimonio,* n. 916; D'Annibale, *Summula,* I, n. 83 nota 8; cf. Langonio, Votum—*Anal. Eccl.* Vol. XIII (1905), p. 385.

[2] Lehmkuhl, *Theologia Moralis,* II, n. 889; Laurentius, *Institutiones, Juris Eccl.,* n. 584; cf. Wernz, Votum—*Anal. Eccl.,* Vol. VII (1899). p. 66 ff.

[3] C. 3 *de sepult.,* III, 12 in VI°: "Is qui habet domicilium in civitate vel castro . . .."

[4] Cf. Fourneret, *Le Domicile Matrimonial,* p. 160 ff.

[5] Deschamps—*Can. Contemp.* Vol. XXIII (1900), p. 385 ff., esp. p. 401; Lombardi, *Institutiones Juris Canon. Privati,* Vol. III, p. 188.

impetus as a result of the indefinite wording of the decree *"Ne Temere,"* regarding the place of marriage.[6] The Code has very definitely settled the matter. The domicile in the city finds no place in the new legislation. The parochial and the diocesan domicile and quasi-domicile alone are recognized. A domicile or quasi-domicile acquired in a parish or quasi-parish[7] is called a parochial domicile; a domicile or quasi-domicile acquired in a diocese, vicariate or prefecture apostolic, but not in a particular parish is called a diocesan domicile.[8] Although, according to the strict wording of the Code in Canon 92, a man who has a parochial domicile has not a diocesan domicile as such, the difference between the two is really one of expression. Residence in a parish with the intention of remaining there permanently involves similar residence and intention in regard to the diocese, and although such residence does not, according to the Code, give one a diocesan domicile, it will give him a domicile in a diocese. In practice, as far as concerns diocesan rights and obligations, the two will amount to the same thing.

The new legislation regarding the place of domicile and quasi-domicile is quite clear and needs little comment. One point, however, may be noted. The place of one's domicile or quasi-domicile as far as the law is concerned, is not the home in which one resides, but the

---

[6] *Il Monitore Ecclesiastico,* 2 series Vol. X, p. 91; cf. Chelodi *"Jus Matrimoniale,"* n. 134.

[7] Canon 216 § 3: "The parts of a diocese are called parishes . . . the parts of an apostolic vicariate or prefecture, if a special rector has been assigned to them, are called quasi parishes."

[8] Cf. cn. 215 § 2: "In jure nomine diocesis venit quoque abbatia vel prelatura nullius."

parish or diocese in which the house is situated. The domicile is attached to the parish or the diocese, and not necessarily to any particular residence. Therefore, in acquiring a domicile or quasi-domicile it is not necessary that one's intention of remaining be directed to a particular house; it is sufficient that one have the intention of remaining in the parish or the diocese. Similarly, when there is question of losing a domicile, one does not lose this domicile until he actually and finally leaves the parish or the diocese.

In connection with the place of domicile, the ancient and time-honored problem of the house situated on the confines of two parishes still presents itself. The general rule is that the house and consequently the domicile, is in that parish in which the entrance is situated.[9] In the event that the house has two entrances each in a different parish, the house is considered to be in that parish in which the principal and more frequented entrance is situated.[10] This latter rule suffers an exception in the event of the dismembration or division of a parish. In this case the Bishop can ascribe the house to a certain parish, even though the principal entrance is not situated in that parish.[11] If it should happen that the only entrance or the principal entrance has been changed by private authority i. e., by the individual, a distinction must be made. If the house has been entirely rebuilt, or changed and en-

---

[9] S. C. C. *Jurisdictionis Parochialis,* 12 Dec. 1874—*A.S.S.* VIII, p. 149; S. R. Rota, *Juris. Paroch.,* 14 May 1912—*Decisiones S. R. Rotae,* IV, Dec. 19, n. 3; De Meester, *"Compendium"* I, n. 320.

[10] Cf. De Meester *l. c.,* and the decisions quoted in the preceding note.

[11] S. C. Ep. et Reg., 14 March 1890—*A.S.S.* XXIII, p. 340; *Collationes Brugenses,* V (1900), p. 688 ff.; De Meester, *l. c.*

larged in greater part, with the entrance opening into a different parish than before, the house is transferred into the second parish. If the entrance to the house alone is changed, the house remains in the original parish.[12] What has been said up to this is the common and certain teaching of canonists, and has been confirmed by the practice of the Roman Congregations. To proceed further would involve one only in doubts and conjectures; and where doubts arise in so delicate a matter as parochial rights, it would seem best to appeal to the ordinary and abide by his decision.

[12] S. R. Rota, *Juris. Paroch.*, 14 May 1912—*Decisiones S. R. Rotae,* IV dec. 19, n. 4; *Collationes Brugenses, l. c.;* De Meester, *l. c.*

CHAPTER XI

THE EFFECTS OF DOMICILE AND QUASI-DOMICILE

From the very beginning of their introduction into the realm of law, whether Roman or Canon Law, the domicile and the quasi-domicile have been the important links, the bonds, attaching the individual with his legal belongings to a certain well-defined territory. By virtue of this legal bond the individual person became subject to the local territorial laws and jurisdiction, and was entitled to the free exercise of his legal rights and obligations under the guidance and protection of the local law.

In Roman law the place to which one became attached by domicile was the local city or municipality; and the law of that municipality was the law to which one thereby became subject. The individual inhabitant (*incola*) had to perform the public *munera* of his own municipality, and here also did he enjoy the advantages of municipal life.[1]

In the Canon Law before the publication of the Code, the place to which the individual became attached by domicile or quasi-domicile was the parish or the diocese; and the particular law of that diocese was the law to which he became subject. The domicile and quasi-domicile also designated one's immediate superiors—the proper pastor and ordinary, under whose jurisdiction the individual person came, and who were to gov-

[1] Cf. page 77.

ern and minister to the individual in the exercise of his Christian rights and obligations, e. g., in regard to the reception of the sacraments, granting of dispensations, ecclesiastical burial.[2]

As was to be expected, the Code of Canon Law has not lessened the importance of the domicile and the quasi-domicile in matters of ecclesiastical discipline. A full and detailed discussion of the effects of domicile and quasi-domicile is beyond the scope of this book. The general principles enunciated in Canon 94 will alone be considered.

Canon 94, §1.—Sive per domicilium sive per quasi-domicilium suum quisque parochum et ordinarium sortitur.

The above regulation tells us that the proper pastor and ordinary of the individual is determined by his domicile or quasi-domicile in the respective parish or diocese. This is the most general and fundamental effect of domicile and quasi-domicile. From it, as veins from a main artery, flow the particular effects that are treated in the different parts of the Code. In general, the domicile and quasi-domicile determine the proper forum,[3] and the particular diocesan law to which a person is subject.[4] They determine the proper pastor in regard to the administration of many sacraments;[5] in regard to ecclesiastical burial;[6] and in re-

[2] Cf. page 65.

[3] Canon 1561.

[4] Canons 13-14.

[5] Canons 738, 484, 854, 938, 1097 § 1° 2°; In regard to lawful assistance at marriage, besides the domicile and quasi-domicile, a month's residence in a place is also sufficient that the pastor of that place be regarded as the proper pastor.

[6] Canons 1216 et seq.

gard to the granting of some dispensations.[7] Finally, they determine the proper ordinary for the administration of some sacraments[8] and for the granting or communicating of many favors and dispensations.[9] The law in general makes no distinction between the domicile and the quasi-domicile as far as the pastor is concerned, and therefore the pastor of one's domicile has no more power nor claim on the individual than the pastor of one's quasi-domicile. In the event, therefore, that one has both a domicile and a quasi-domicile, it is he, not the pastor who may decide, for example, from whom he wishes to receive the sacraments.[10] In most respects, this rule is true also of the ordinary of domicile and quasi-domicile. There is, however, one exception. In determining the proper bishop for the lawful reception of Orders, the quasi-domicile is entirely insufficient. The domicile, and that alone, determines the proper bishop of the candidate for Orders.[11] The Code has determined nothing new in this matter. The insufficiency of the quasi-domicile in determining the proper bishop for orders has always been a principle of Canon Law.[12] In connection with the domicile for purposes of ordination one point must be mentioned. As in the preceding legislation a qualified domicile is required in determining the proper bishop for licit reception of Orders. In addition to the possession of

---

[7] Canon 1245.

[8] Canons 783; 956.

[9] Canons 82; 1028; 1245; 1313.

[10] Augustine, *"A Commentary on Canon Law,"* II, p. 18.

[11] Canon 956.

[12] C. 3, *de tem.; ordin.*, I, 11, in sexto; Innocent XII Const. *"Speculatores,"* 4 Nov. 1694—*Fontes* n. 258; Alberti, *De domicilio ecclesiastico*, p. 36.

the ordinary domicile one of two conditions must be fulfilled. The place of domicile of the candidate must also be the place of origin *or* the candidate must—with exceptions mentioned in Canon 956—declare on oath that he intends to remain permanently in the diocese. The difference between the qualified domicile of Canon 956 and that of the Constitution "*Speculatores*" is clear.[13]

In the event that a person may have many proper pastors and ordinaries by reason of the fact that he has two or more domiciles or quasi-domiciles, he is free to choose whichever he wills, unless this is forbidden by law.[14] The law does restrict this choice in two cases in connection with ecclesiastical burial.[15] In the other cases, in which the law does not restrict the person's freedom of choice, it is fitting that he select the pastor or the ordinary of the proper parish or diocese in which he is actually staying.[16]

Canon 94, §2.—Proprius vagi parochus vel ordinarius est parochus vel ordinarius loci in quo actu commorantur.

This principle has put an end to two controversies that existed before the Code. The first controversy arose in connection with the proper pastor of *vagi* in regard to assistance at marriage. A number of canonists[17] declared that any pastor in the world could

---

[13] Cf. page 60.

[14] Epitome, I, 186; Bouuaert-Simenon, *Manuale,* n. 246; Coronata, *Institutiones* n. 124.

[15] Canons 1216 § 2; Canon 1218 § 1, § 2.

[16] Maroto, *l. c.;* Bouuaert-Simenon, *l. c.*

[17] Sanchez, *De Matrimonio,* III, 25, n. 11 ff.; St. Alphonsus, *Theologia Moralis,* l. VI, n. 1089.

assist or delegate another to assist at the marriage of *vagi*. For example, a certain *vagus* is at present staying in the parish of St. Ann. According to these canonists, the parish priest of St. Mary's or St. Paul's may come to St. Ann's to assist at the marriage.[18] Another group of canonists declared that the pastor of the place in which the *vagus* was actually staying was alone competent to assist at the marriage.[19] This latter opinion was regarded as the more probable, but the former was regarded as at least probable.[20] The Code has clearly decided matters. The proper pastor of *vagi* is the pastor of the place in which they are actually staying.[21]

The second controversy arose in connection with the subjection of *vagi* to the particular laws of the place in which they were actually staying. Some authorities declared that *vagi* were not bound by the particular laws of the territory, except in the case of laws passed especially for *vagi*.[22] Other canonists asserted that *vagi* were bound by the particular laws of the place in which they were staying.[23] The Code has sounded the death-knell of the first opinion. This is clear from the general principle laid down in the present canon. Canon 14 §2 removes all doubt on the point.[24] The

[18] Cf. Gasparri, *De Matrimonio*, n. 917.

[19] Schmalzgruber, l. IV, tit, III, n. 862; Gasparri, *l. c.;* Wernz, *Jus Decretalium,* IV, n. 178, nota 193.

[20] Alberti, *"De domicilio ecclesiastico,"* p. 44; Wernz, *l. c.;* Gasparri, *l. c.*

[21] Canon 94 § 2.

[22] Wernz, *Jus Decretalium,* I, n. 107; Alberti, *op. cit.,* p. 16.

[23] Sanchez, *in Decal.,* l. I, c. 12, 13; D'Annibale, *Summula,* I, n. 86, nota 42; D'Angelo, *Il domicilio ecclesiastico,* p. 46 ff.

[24] Canon 14 § 2: "Vagi obligantur legibus tam generalibus tam particularibus quae vigent in loco quo versantur."

phrase *actu commorantur* in Canon 94, presents some difficulty. This phrase immediately calls to mind a distinction between *vagi actu itinerantes* and *vagi* having a *sedes commorationis* that is contained in Canon 1097. Certainly where there is question of *vagi actu itinerantes,* there will be no difficulty. The pastor of the place in which they are *hic et nunc* is their proper pastor. But what about those *vagi* who have some place of residence, a *sedes commorationis?* Suppose they have this *sedes commorationis* in parish A, but at the present moment they are in parish B. Who is their proper pastor? To make the matter concrete let us take a typical example. Paul and Mary, both *vagi,* are residing in parish A, where they have been for the past three weeks. They decide to get married. Must they go to the pastor of A for the marriage, or can they simply approach any neighboring pastor? A number of authorities[25] declare that the pastor of the place in which these *vagi* have their *sedes commorationis* is alone competent to assist at the marriage. Vidal[26] reaches this conclusion on the strength of the distinction made in Canon 1097 between the *vagi actu itinerantes* and the *vagi* having *sedes commorationis.* The distinction and conclusion of Vidal, defended also by Vlaming[27] and Tanquerey,[28] have been confirmed by a decision of the Rota in a recent matrimonial case.[29]

---

[25] Vidal, *Jus Canonicum,* V, n. 541, nota 55; Vlaming, *Praelectiones juris Matr.* n. 580; Tanquerey, *"Synopsis Theologiae Moralis,"* n. 920.

[26] *L. c.*

[27] *L. c.*

[28] *L. c.*

[29] S. R. Rota *in Causa Ravennaten,* 29 Dec. 1911—*A.A.S.,* IV (1912), 330.

In the course of this decision, it was declared that a certain woman, a *vaga,* had her actual residence in a house situated outside the territory of the parish in which the marriage in question had taken place.[80] Clearly then the *actualis commoratio* was not verified in the place in which the woman had gone merely to contract marriage. The opinion of Vidal is also favored by the interpretation generally given to the phrase *actualis commoratio* by canonists. According to this interpretation this phrase indicates a residence for some time, e.g., a few days or a week at least, not a mere passing stay *"per modum omnino obiter transeuntis."*[81] It would seem then, that this opinion, solidly supported as it is by authority, may, by virtue of Canon 20, supply a norm which, in the absence of any contrary opinion, be regarded as certain.

A final point in connection with *vagi* concerns those who have no domicile or quasi-domicile, but only a month's residence in some parish or diocese. Before the Code, by virtue of a decree of the Congregation of the Sacraments,[82] those only were considered *vagi* in matrimonial matters who had neither a proper pastor nor a proper ordinary by reason of a domicile or a month's residence. Those persons, therefore, who had at least a month's residence in a place were not classed as *vagi.* This regulation, exempting those who have

[80] S. R. Rota, *Causa Ravennaten,* 29 Dec. 1911, *l. c.*: "Sponsa tempore matrimonii *actualiter* commorabatur Florentiae, idque in quodam diversorio, quod insuper extra territorium illius paroeciae situm erat, in cujus finibus matrimonium contractum erat."

[81] Cf. Cappello, *De Matrimonio,* n. 686; Wouters, "De Forma *Promissionis et Celebrationis Matrimonii,"* p. 34-5; Rossi, *"De Celebratione Matrimonii,"* n. 56; Vlaming, op. cit., n. 72; Damen, *"Theologia Moralis,"* II, n. 840.

[82] S. C. de Sacr., 13 March 1910—*A.A.S.,* II (1910), 193 ff.

only a month's residence in a place from the category of *vagi*, is entirely opposed to the present law of the Code as enunciated in Canon 91, and by virtue of Canon 6, 1°, it must be regarded as abrogated.

Canon 91 defines a *vagus* as one who has no domicile or quasi-domicile anywhere. But a person who has only a month's residence in a place, obviously has not a domicile or quasi-domicile. In the new legislation, therefore, a person who has only a month's residence in a place is a *vagus*.

Canon 94, §3.—Illorum qui non habent nisi diocesanum domicilium vel quasi-domicilium, proprius parochus est parochus loci in quo actu commorantur.

Although, by virtue of Canon 91, those who have a diocesan domicile only are not classed as *vagi*, they are, practically speaking, in the same position as *vagi* as far as their relations with the different parishes of the diocese are concerned. The regulation, therefore, in the preceding section concerning *vagi* in general is to be applied to those who have only a diocesan domicile, as far as the exercise of their parochial rights and obligations is concerned.

BIBLIOGRAPHY

JURIDICAL SOURCES

Acta Apostolicae Sedis (*AAS*), Romae, 1909—

Acta Sanctae Sedis (*ASS*), 41 Vols., Romae, 1865-1908.

Canones et Decreta Concilii Tridentini, 19 ed., Taurini, 1913.

Codex Iuris Canonici Pii X Pontificis Maximi iussu digestu Benedicti Papae XV auctoritate promulgatus, Romae, 1918.

Codicis Iuris Canonici Fontes, 4 vols., Romae, 1923-1926.

Collectanea Sacrae Congregationis de Propaganda Fide (*Coll.*) 2 vols., Romae, 1907.

Collectio Lacensis, Acta et Decreta Sacrorum Conciliorum Recentiorum (*Coll. Lacen.*), 7 vols., Friburgi Br., 1870-1890.

Concilii Plenarii Baltimorensis II, Acta et Decreta, Baltimore, 1894.

Concilii Plenarii Baltimorensis III, Acta et Decreta, Baltimore, 1884.

Corpus Juris Canonici (Cum glossis), Augustae Taurinorum, 1587-1588.

Corpus Juris Canonici, 2 vols., Lipsiae, 1922.

Corpus Juris Civilis (cum glossis), Lugduni, 1549-1550.

Corpus Juris Civilis, Berolini, 1922.

Denzinger-Bannwart, *Enchiridion Symbolorum Definitionum et Declarationum de Rebus Fidei et Morum,* 14-15 ed., Friburgi Br., 1922.

Mansi, *Sacrorum Conciliorum Nova et Amplissima Collectio,* 51 vols., Paris, 1901-1919.

Sacrae Romanae Rotae Decisiones seu Sententiae, 9 vols., Romae, 1912-

Thesaurus Resolutionum Sacrae Congregationis Concilii, 167 vols., Romae, 1718-1908.

REFERENCE WORKS

Abbas Panormitanus, *Commentaria in quinque libros Decretalium,* 8 vols., Lugduni, 1547.

Aertnys-Damen, *Theologia Moralis,* 2 vols., Taurini, 1928.

Aichner, Simon, *Compendium Juris Ecclesiastici,* 2 ed., Brixiae, 1887.

Alberti, J., *De Domicilio Ecclesiastico,* Romae, 1909.

Alceatus, A., *Opera Omnia*, Basileae, 1582.

Alphonsus, De Liguori, *Theologia Moralis*, 2 vols., Torino, 1867.

Augustine, Charles, *A Commentary on the New Code of Canon Law*, 8 vols., St. Louis, 1918-1922.

Ayrinhac, H. A., *Constitution of the Church in the New Code of Canon Law*, New York, 1925.

Ayrinhac, H. A., *General Legislation in the New Code of Canon Law*, New York, 1923.

Ayrinhac, H. A., *Marriage Legislation in the New Code of Canon Law*, New York, 1918.

Badii, Caesar, *Institutiones Juris Canonici*, 3. ed., 2 vols., Florentiae, 1921.

Ballerini-Palmieri, *Opus Theologicum Morale*, 3. ed., 7 vols., Prati, 1898-1901.

Barbosa, Agostinus, *Tractatus Varii*, Lugduni, 1660.

Bartolus A Saxaferrato, *Opera Omnia*, Venetiis, 1590-1615.

Benedictus XIV, *Institutiones Ecclesiasticae*, 3. ed., 2 vols., Venetiis, 1788.

Blat, Albertus, O. P., *Commentarium Textus Codicis Juris Canonici*, 5 vols., Romae, 1921-1927.

Bonacina, Martinus, *Opera Omnia*, 3 vols., Antverpiae, 1632.

Bonfante, P., *Instituzioni di Diritto Romano*, Milano, 1921.

Brunnemanni, J. *Commentarius in Paudectas*, Coloniae Allobrogum, 1762.

Brunnemanni, J., *Commentarius in Codicem*, Coloniae Allobrogum, 1771.

Brys, J., *Principes de Droit Romain*, Paris, 1927.

Buckland, W. W., *A manual of Roman Private Law*, Cambridge, 1925.

Butler, Chas., *Horae Subsecivae*, London, 1827.

Calvinus, Joannes, *Magnum Lexicon Juridicum*, 2 vols., Coloniae Allobrogum, 1759.

Capello, Felix, *Tractatus Canonico-Moralis de Sacramentis juxta Codicem Juris Canonici*, 3 vols., Taurinorum Augustae, 1927.

Carriere, Josephus, *De Matrimonio*, 2 vols., Parisiis, 1837.

Castropalao, F., *Opus Morale*, 4 vols., Venetiis, 1721.

Catholic Encyclopedia, 16 vols., New York, 1907-1912; Supplement, I, 1922.

Chelodi, Joannes, *Jus De Personis juxta Codicem Juris Canonici*, 2. ed., Tridenti, 1927.

Chelodi, Joannes, *Jus Matrimonale juxta Codicem Juris Canonici*, 3. ed., Tridenti, 1921.

Chelodi, Joannes, *Jus Poenale et Ordo Procedendi in Judiciis criminalibus juxta Codicem Juris Canonici,* Tridenti, 1925.

Claeys-Bouuaert-Simenon, *Manuale Juris Canonici,* 2. ed., Bandae et Leodii, 1926.

Clavasio, Angelo, *Summa-Angelica,* 2 vols., Venetiis, 1525.

Cocchi, Guidus, *Commentarium in Codicem Juris Canonici ad Usum Scholarum,* 3. ed., 8 vols., Taurinorum Augustae, 1925.

Coronata, P. Matthaeus Conte A., O. M. C., *Institutiones Juris Canonici,* vol. I, Taurini, 1928.

Cujas, J., *Opera Omnia,* Venetiis, 1758-1783.

Cuq, Ed., *Institutiones Juridiques des Romains,* 2 vols., Paris, 1891-1902.

D'Angelo, Sosius, *Il Domicilio Ecclesiastico,* Giarre, 1917.

D'Angelo, Sosius, *Jus Digestorum,* Rome, 1927.

D'Annibale, Josephus, *Summula Theologiae Moralis,* 3 vols., Romae, 1896.

De Angelis, Philippus, *Praelectiones Juris Canonici,* 4 vols., Romae Parisiis, 1877-1878.

De Becker, I., *De Sponsalibus et Matrimonio Praelectiones Canonicae,* 2. ed., Louvanii, 1903.

Declareuil, J., *Rome the Law Giver,* London, 1927.

De Meester, A., *Juris Canonici et Juris Canonico-Civilis Compendium,* nova ed., 3 vols. in 4, Brugis, 1921-1928.

Dens, P., *Tractatus de Sponsalibus et Matrimonio,* Mechliniae, 1861.

Dernberg, H., *System des Romischen Rechts,* Berlin, 1911-12.

De Smet, Aloysius, *De Sponsalibus et Matrimonio,* 4. ed., Brugis, 1927.

Dictionaire de Theologie Catholique, Paris, 1903 ff.

Donnellus, H., *Opera Omnia,* Romae, 1828.

Durandus, Guilielmus, *Speculum Juris,* 3 vols., Venetiis, 1577.

Engel, Ludovicus, *Collegium universi juris canonici,* Venetiis, 1760.

Fagnanus, P., *Commentaria in V libros Decretalium,* 3 vols., Venetiis, 1764.

Farren, N., *Domicile and Quasi-domicile,* Dublin, 1920.

Feije, Henricus Joannes, *De Impedimentis et Dispensationibus Matrimonialibus,* 3. ed., Louvanii, 1885.

Ferraris, Lucius F., *Bibliotheca Prompta Canonica, Juridica, Moralis Theologica,* 8 vols., Romae, 1885.

Ferreres, Joannes B., *Compendium Theologiae Moralis ad Normam Codicis Juris Canonici,* 7. ed., 2 vols., Barcinone, 1928.

Ferrini, C., *Pandette,* Milano, 1917.

Festus, Sextus P., *De Verborum significatione libri XX*, 2 vols., London, 1826.

Fourneret, P., *Le Domicile Matrimonial*, Paris, 1906.

Funk, F. X., *A Manual of Church History*, 2 vols., London, 1910.

Gasparri, Henry, *De Domicilio et Quasi-domicilio*, Romae, 1897.

Gasparri, Petrus, *Tractatus Canonicus de Matrimonio*, 2. ed., 2 vols., Parisiis, 1892.

Gasparri, Petrus, *Tractatus Canonicus de Sacra Ordinatione*, 2 vols., Paris, 1893.

Gellius, Aulus, *Attic Nights*, translated by John C. Rolfe, 3 vols., London, 1927-1928.

Gennari, C., *Quistioni Canoniche*, Roma, 1908.

Gobat, G., *Opera Moralia*, Venetiis, 1749.

Gonzalez, Tellez, Emmanuel, *Commentaria in quinque libros Decretalium*, 5 vols., Lugduni, 1693.

Hostiensis, *Commentaria in quinque libros Decretalium*, 3 vols., Venetiis, 1581.

Huberi, Ner., *Praelectiones Juris Civilis*, 3 vols., Maceratae, 1838-9.

Konings-Putzer, *Commentarium in Facultates Apostolicas*, 5. ed., New York, 1898.

La Croix, C., *Theologia Moralis*, 2 vols., Mediolani, 1724.

Laurentius, J., *Institutiones Juris Ecclesiasticae*, Friburgi Briscoviae, 1908.

Laymann, Paulus, *Theologia Moralis*, 5 vols. in 1, *Lutetiae Parisiorum*, 1627.

Leage, R. W., *Roman Private Law*, London, 1924.

Lega, Michael, *Praelectiones in Textum Juris Canonici de Judiciis Ecclesiastici*, vol. I., Romae, 1905.

Lehmkuhl, Augustinus, *Theologia Moralis*, 5. ed., 2 vols., Friburgi Brisgoviae, 1897.

Leurenius, Petrus, S. J., *Forum Ecclesiasticum de Universo Jure Canonico*, 5 vols., Venetiis, 1729.

Lombardi, C., *Juris Canonici Privati Institutiones*, 2. ed., 3 vols., Romae, 1901.

Many, S., *Praelectiones de Sacra Ordinatione*, Paris, 1905.

Maroto, Philippus, *Institutiones Juris Canonici ad Normam Novi Codicis*, 3. ed., 2 vols., Romae, 1921.

Maschardus, Josephus, *Conclusiones Probationum Omnium*, 3 vols., Venetiis, 1593.

Maschat, Remigius, *Institutiones Canonicae*, 2 vols., Romae, 1757.

Menochius, Jacobus, *De presumptionibus, Conjecturis, Signis et Indiciis Commentaria*, 2 vols., Coloniae Allobrogum, 1684.

Morey, William C., *Outlines of Roman Law,* 2 ed., New York, London, 1913.

Muniz, T., *Derecho Parroquial,* 2 vols., Sevilla, 1923.

Navarrus, *Opera,* Romae, 1590.

Navarrus, *Consilia,* Coloniae Aggripinae, 1616.

Noldin, H., *Decretum de Sponsalibus et Matrimonio,* Oeniponte, 1911.

Ojetti, B., *Commentarium in Codicem Juris Canonici,* vol. I, Romae, 1927.

Ojetti, B., *Synopsis Rerum Moralium et Juris Pontificii,* Romae, 1909.

Ortolan, M., *History of Roman Law,* London, 1871.

Passerini, *Commentarium in Librum Sextum Decretalium,* 3 vols., Venetiis, 1698.

Phillimore, Robert, *The Law of Domicile,* Philadelphia, 1847.

Pignatelli, J., *Consultationes Canonicae,* 11 vols., Coloniae Allobrogum, 1700.

Pirhing, Enricus, *Jus Canonicum Novo Methodo Explicatum,* ed. novissima, 5 vols., Dilingae, 1722.

Pontius, Basilius, *De Sacramento Matrimonii Tractatus,* Bruxellis, 1627.

Prierias, Sylvester, *Summa Sylvestrina,* 2 vols.

Prummer, Dominicus M., *Manuale Juris Canonici in Usum Clericorum Praesertim Illorum qui ad Instituta Religiosa Pertinent,* 3. ed., Friburgi Brisgoviae, 1922.

Raymundus de Pennafort, *Summa,* Veronae, 1744.

Reiffenstuel, Anacletus, *Jus Canonicum Universum,* 4 vols., Venetiis, 1735.

Rigantius, Josephus B., *Commentarium in Regulas, Constitutiones et Ordinationes Cancelariae Apostolicae,* 4 vols. in 2 Coloniae Allobrogum, 1751.

Sanchez, Thomas, *De Sancto Matrimonii Sacramento Disputationum,* 3 vols., Lugduni, 1669.

Santamaria, *Commentarios al Codigo Canonico,* Vol. I, Madrid, 1920.

Santi, Franciscus, *Praelectiones Juris Canonici juxta Ordinem Decretalium,* 5 vols. in 2, Ratisbonae, 1886.

Savigny, F. C. von, *System des Heutigen Romischen Rechts,* 8 vols., Berlin, 1849.

Schmalzgrueber, R. P. Franciscus, *Jus Ecclesiasticum Universum,* 12 vols., Romae, 1843-1845.

Sherman, Chas. P., *Roman Law in the Modern World,* 3 vols., New York, 1924.

Soglia, Joannes, *Institutiones Juris Publici Ecclesiastici,* Parisiis, 1842.

Suarez, F., *Opera Omnia,* Venetiis, 1740-1757.

Tanquerey, Adrianus, *Synopsis Theologiae Moralis et Pastoralis ad mentem S. Thomae et S. Alphonsi Hodiernis Moribus Accomodata,* 8 ed., 3 vols., Romae, 1921.

Thomassinus, L., *Vetus et Nova Ecclesiae Disciplina Circa Beneficia et Beneficiarios,* 3 vols., Parisiis, 1688.

Toso, *Ad Codicem Juris Canonici. . . Commentaria Minora,* Romae, 1921.

Universa Civilis et Criminalis Jurisprudentia, 12 vols., Taurini, 1824-1829.

Van de Burgt, F. P., *Tractatus de Dispensationibus Matrimonialibus,* Sylvae Ducis, 1885.

Vecchiotti, Septimus M., *Institutiones Canonicae,* 16. ed., 3 vols., Augustae Taurinorum, 1875.

Vermeersch-Creusen, *Epitome Juris Canonici cum Commentariis ad Scholas et ad Usum Privatum,* 3 ed., 3 vols., Mechliniae Romae, 1927.

Vidal, P., *Institutiones Juris Civilis Romani,* Rome, 1915.

Vlaming, Th. M., *Praelectiones Juris Matrimonii ad Normam Codicis Juris Canonici,* 3. ed., 2 vols., Bussum in Hollandia, 1919-1921.

Wernz, Franciscus Xav., *Jus Decretalium ad Usum Praelectionum in Scholis Textus Canonici sive Juris Decretalium,* Vol. I, II, Prati, 1913-1915.

Wernz-Vidal, *Jus Canonicum, auctore P. Francisco Xav. Wernz, S. I. ad Codicis Norman Exactum opera P. Petri Vidal,* Vol. II, V, VI, Romae, 1927-1928.

Whittuck, E. A.—Poste, E., *Gai Institutiones Juris Civilis,* Oxford, 1904.

Windscheid, B., *Lehrbuch des Pandectenrechts,* 3 vols., Dusseldorf, 1875.

Woywod, Stanislaus, *A Practical Commentary on the Code of Canon Law,* 2 vols., New York, 1925.

Zallinger, J., *Institutiones Juris Ecclesiastici maxime privati, ordine Decretalium,* Romae, 1832.

PERIODICALS

American Ecclestiastical Review, The (AER), Philadelphia, 1889—

Apollinaris, Romae, 1928—

Archiv fur katholisches Kirchenrecht (AkKR), Innsbruck, 1857—

Commentarium pro Religiosis (CpR), Romae, 1920—
Gregorianum, Commentarii de Re Theologica et Philosophica, Romae, 1920—
Il Monitore Ecclesiastico (ME), Romae, 1888—
Irish Ecclesiastical Record, the (IER), Dublin, 1865
Irish Theological Quarterly, 1905-1921.
Jus Pontificium, Romae, 1921—
Le Canoniste Contemporain, Paris, 1878—
Nouvelle Revue Theologique (NRT), Paris, 1856—
Periodica, de Re Canonica et Morali, Romae et Brugis, 1905—

Universitas Catholica Americae

WASHINGTON, D. C.

FACULTAS JURIS CANONICI

1930

No. 60

DEUS LUX MEA

TITULI

QUOS

AD DOCTORATUS GRADUM

IN

JURE CANONICO

APUD UNIVERSITATEM CATHOLICAM AMERICAE

CONSEQUENDUM

PUBLICE PROPUGNABIT

JOANNES M. COSTELLO

SACERDOS ARCHIDIOECESIS

NEO-EBORACENSIS

JURIS CANONICI LICENTIATUS

HORA XI AM DIE XXIV MAII MCMXXX

TITULI

DE JURE CANONICO

I.	De Dissertatione.	
II.	De Historia Juris Canonici.	
III.	Canones 1-7	De Ambitu Codicis.
IV.	Canones 8-24	De Legibus Ecclesiasticis.
V.	Canones 25-30	De Consuetudine.
VI.	Canones 31-35	De Temporis Supputatione.
VII.	Canones 63-79	De Privilegiis.
VIII.	Canones 80-86	De Dispensationibus.
IX.	Canones 87-107	Generales Notiones de Personis.
X.	Canones 111-117	De Clericorum Aescriptione Alicui Diocesi.
XI.	Canones 118-123	De Juribus et Privilegiis Clericorum
XII.	Canones 124-144	De Obligationibus Clericorum.
XIII.	Canones 145-195	De Officiis Ecclesiasticis.
XIV.	Canones 196-210	De Potestate Ordinaria et Delegata.
XV.	Canones 211-214	De Reductione Clericorum ad Statum Laicalem.
XVI.	Canones 487-498	De Notione Religionis, et de Erectione et Suppressione Religionis, Provinciae, Domus.
XVII.	Canones 499-537	De Religionum Regimine.
XVIII.	Canones 538-586	De Admissione in Religionem.
XIX.	Canones 587-591	De Ratione Studiorum in Religionibus Clericalibus.
XX.	Canones 592-631	De Obligationibus et Privilegiis Religiosorum.
XXI.	Canones 632-672	De Transitu ad Aliam Religionem, de Egressu e Religione, et de Dimissione Religiosorum.
XXII.	Canones 673-681	De Societatibus sive Virorum sive Mulierum in Communi Viventium Sine Votis.
XXIII.	Canones 1012-1018	De Matrimonio in Genere.
XXIV.	Canones 1019-1034	De Iis quae Matrimonii Celebrationi Praemitti Debent.

Tituli

XXV.	Canones 1035-1057	De Impedimentis in Genere.
XXVI.	Canones 1058-1066	De Impedimentis Impedientibus.
XXVII.	Canones 1067-1080	De Impedimentis Dirimentibus.
XXVIII.	Canones 1081-1093	De Consensu Matrimoniali.
XXIX.	Canones 1552-1568	De Notione Judicii et de Foro Competenti.
XXX.	Canones 1569-1607	De Variis Tribunalium Gradibus et Speciebus.
XXXI.	Canones 1608-1645	De Disciplina in Tribunalibus Servanda.
XXXII.	Canones 1646-1666	De Partibus in Causa.
XXXIII.	Canones 1667-1705	De Actionibus et Exceptionibus.
XXXIV.	Canones 1706-1725	De Causae Introductione.
XXXV.	Canones 1726-1746	De Litis Contestatione, de Litis Instantia, et de Interrogationibus Partibus in Judicio Faciendis.
XXXVI.	Canones 1747-1836	De Probationibus.
XXXVII.	Canones 1837-1857	De Causis Incidentibus.
XXXVIII.	Canones 1858-1877	De Processus Publicatione, de Conclusione in Causa, de Causae Discussione, et de Sententia.
XXXIX.	Canones 2195-2198	De Natura Delicti Ejusque Divisione.
XL.	Canones 2199-2211	De Imputabilitate Delicti, de Causis Illam Aggravantibus vel Minuentibus, et de Juridicis Delicti Effectibus.
XLI.	Canones 2212-2213	De Conatu Delicti.
XLII.	Canones 2214-2240	De Poenis in Genere.
XLIII.	Canones 2241-2285	De Poenis Medicinalibus seu de Censuris.
XLIV.	Canones 2286-2305	De Poenis Vindicativis.
XLV.	Canones 2306-2313	De Remediis Poenalibus et Poenitentiis.
XLVI.	The Periods of Roman Law.	
XLVII.	The Sources of Roman Law.	
XLVIII.	Personality.	
XLIX.	Slavery.	
L.	Citizenship.	
LI.	Patria Potestas.	
LII.	Personae in Manu.	
LIII.	Personae in Mancipio.	
LIV.	Tutela et Cura.	
LV.	Ownership.	

Tituli

LVI. De Obligationibus in Genere.
LVII. De Obligationibus Extra-Contractualibus.
LVIII. Furtum.
LIX. Damnum Injuria Datum.
LX. Injuria.

Vidit Facultas:
PHILIPPUS BERNARDINI, S.T.D., J.U.D.,
Decanus.

LUDOVICUS H. MOTRY, S.T.D., J.C.D.,
a Secretis.

VALENTINUS T. SCHAAF, O.F.M., J.C.D.

FRANCISCUS J. LARDONE, S.T.D., J.U.D.

Vidit Rector Magnificus Universitatis:
JACOBUS HUGO RYAN, Ph.D., S.T.D.

VITA

John Michael Costello was born in New York City on November 16, 1903. He attended the parochial school of Our Lady of Good Counsel, and received his high school and college training in Cathedral College, New York City. He entered St. Joseph's Seminary, Dunwoodie, New York, in September, 1922, and was ordained to the Priesthood on June 2, 1928. In October of that year, he entered the Catholic University of America at Washington, D. C., and registered in the School of Canon Law.

www.ingramcontent.com/pod-product-compliance
Lightning Source LLC
LaVergne TN
LVHW050239080826
844660LV00012B/560

* 9 7 8 0 8 1 3 2 2 2 4 9 3 *